Win Them Over *FASTER*

Win them OVER FASTER

Dynamic Techniques for College Adjuncts and New Faculty

14 Essential Skills for College Teaching Success

Patricia Linehan, Ph.D.

Win Them Over Faster
Dynamic Techniques for College Adjuncts and New Faculty
14 Essential Skills. Updated Edition
by Patricia Linehan, Ph.D

Copyright © 2015, Patricia Linehan
Mixed Pack Press an imprint of Another Life, LLC
57105 Deerhaven Dr, Mankato, MN 56001

Cover and text design by Bright Light Graphics, *www.brightlightgraphics.com*

LCCN 2015913282

Linehan, Patricia, 1950-
Win Them Over Faster: Dynamic Techniques for College Adjuncts and New
Faculty. 14 Essential Skills. Updated Edition
p. cm.
Includes bibliographical references.
ISBN 978-0-9966508-0-9

Dedicated to my husband, Terry Clodfelter, Lt. Col USAFRR,
my best friend and a stellar college teacher.
Thanks for helping with so many ideas and all your support.

To my children, Isaac, Ezra and Ira.
I may have been your first teacher, but you are my constant teachers
and I am grateful.

WHY YOU SHOULD READ THIS BOOK

First, the noble reasons:

A.   Because you want to be the best teacher possible.

B.   Because students deserve the best teachers.

Academic program reviews frequently measure quality of teaching by faculty credentials, but students measure quality of teaching quite differently. They *assume* their instructor knows the subject; after all, they're paying to be taught by experts. They want *more than the degree;* they want invigorating, dynamic instruction that interests them and keeps them stimulated, updated, and very far from bored.

Second, the practical reason: Your JOB.

Administrators know quality of teaching influences retention – an issue they are very concerned about.

Instructors in postsecondary institutions are expected to use active learning techniques and varied means of assessment. Both work better than straight lectures and big tests to help students learn, particularly for the diversity of students enrolled in colleges. Deans and search committees know this. And so do our students, who are extremely intolerant of being bored.

Becoming a top quality teacher may mean more job security for you.

Third, get your questions answered.

I have been teaching college teachers how to teach, assess, and develop curriculum for many years. Over those years I collected questions. What I found is whether we are in the liberal arts or teaching welding to diploma students, we have a lot of the same issues. Questions like
*   How can I get students to class?
*   How can I get them to prepare ahead of time?
*   How do I grade fairly but quickly?

- How do I grade group work?
- How do I handle bored students during lectures?
- How do I get students more curious and involved in class?
- Should I grade on attendance?
- Why don't students apply what they are learning?
- How can I get them to think? Pay attention? Ask questions? Join discussions?

My goal is to answer your questions.

An Important Note

This book is a *practical application* of current thought and research on college teaching. It is not a research report or a literature review, so it isn't filled with internal citations.

My goal is simply this: *to help you be an engaging, effective teacher as quickly as possible.*

When you want to explore the research references behind my recommendations you'll find them at the end of the book.

WELCOME TO THE WORLD
OF COLLEGE TEACHING
And Hurry Up, Your Class is About to Start!

If you had two or three months to prepare your classes, lucky lucky you! But chances are pretty good you've had far less time – maybe two weeks? Two days? For my first adjunct position at a Big Ten institution, I had a whole twelve days to prepare. I was handed a thick textbook and an exceedingly sketchy sample syllabus, and although I had no teaching experience at all, that was it for any help! My office was my car. I knew no one. I didn't have a clue even what questions to ask. I was on my own.

The first day of class my hands shook holding the syllabus. I wanted to do a fabulous job, but I'm sure I didn't. I had the right degree and the right desire but very few tools beyond the lecture and test and class discussion (which frankly went poorly). Those tools were standard for the times, but today these strategies are not enough.

After almost three decades in higher education as a teacher and administrator, I now know a lot more about teaching, assessment, and class organization. I also know quality teaching impacts how students think and feel about their college, which is a particular concern for teachers and administrators with retention in mind. Colleges want teachers whose classroom skills help retain students.

But teaching was probably not the focus of the degree that helped you land this current job. And having a Masters or Ph.D. or twenty years of industry experience doesn't assure someone can teach. Our students are fairly demanding consumers. They want classroom environments designed to engage them. Like it or not, that's the reality.

The other reality is this: in most fields there is a stack of applicants for each position. You must stand out to get your foot in the door – and once it is wedged in there you have to be a good teacher to stay. Luckily for us, teaching is far more "skill" than "art." Skills can be learned.

The little book in your hands is based on two things: educational psychology research and decades of experience. I wish *Win Them Over Faster* had been available when I took my first teaching job because it would have given me both hope and skills. I firmly believe new instructors can become great teachers very quickly. They do not have to learn from painful trial and error over many semesters. Besides, students want an effective instructor – *right now*. I want to help you be that instructor.

Teaching is still one of the best jobs in the world! Learn to do it well and you will enjoy watching your students thrive!

Patricia L. Linehan Ph.D.

TABLE OF CONTENTS

REALITY CHECK FOR
ADJUNCT INSTRUCTORS

Personal contacts and relationships help you get first jobs. It's competitive out there. You have to be willing to market yourself. I know many faculty who taught adjunct for years before landing a full time position. So being adjunct is a bit like fishing: you have to decide if you want to dangle one worm in the water or cast a big net. If adjunct teaching is a hobby, cast a worm. If you are doing this in order to pay rent and you really want a fulltime position, build multiple webs of relationships. Here are some suggestions to help you find the positions you want:

- Don't just answer higher ed ads or openings posted on college websites. Send resumes to all schools within commuting distance. Include great cover letters. Find out the real decision maker's name for your area and address your information to her/him.
- Make sure your materials fit the individual needs and mission of the college. Yes, that means slight adjustments over and over, but it is worth your time. I have been on many a search committee that wondered why an applicant would send his/her lengthy publishing list and detailed research interests to a community and technical college. I have seen sloppy "cut and paste" jobs where only *some* college names were changed from a previous use of the same cover letter, indicating the same application was going out to numerous places and wasn't tailored to our school's mission.
- After sending materials, do follow-up phone calls asking to meet and talk with the VP, dean, or chair – whoever hires. Assure them you won't take much of their time. Your face and smile will come to mind for a last-minute "crisis hire."
- Always follow up those meetings with a brief thank you note – if your handwriting is legible and you don't have spelling or grammar errors. Thank you notes will probably not sway anyone into hiring you if you aren't a good candidate, but in a pool with many equal fish, a polite note may indeed help.
- Don't be a snob about where you'll teach. Public? Private? For-profit? Two-year? Four-year? All teaching experience is helpful. The more types of colleges you teach at the more you can honestly say you have experience with diverse groups. This is important.
- Seek out instructors and administrators at local conferences and chat. Establish relationships. Present at those conferences; show your competence.

- Find out the hiring schedule for each school. Then call well before decisions are made. There is a cycle for hiring.
- Let the hiring VP, dean, or chair know you are available on short notice, for "crisis hires." Remind them every now and then. You don't want to be a pest, but all these people understand the adjunct's situation. Many of them started their careers in your shoes.
- Keep all your contact information updated at each school so you can be reached. If something changes, this is another valid reason to send a brief note and make another contact.
- Answer calls immediately! For a last-minute hire, deans will probably be calling a stack of candidates and leaving messages if no one answers. First come, first hired.
- When you send out a resume and cover letter, make sure they are flawless. I cannot tell you how many times I have seen search committee members toss a vitae with a couple of proofing errors into the look-at-last pile. Right or wrong, that's reality.
- Personal contact will help keep adjunct classes coming your way. Keep in contact with your hiring authority once you get a class. Be visible. If she or he invites you to a meeting or an in-service for professional development, go! Be sure to say Hi! Many adjuncts are invited to in-services, but few arrive. Be the exception.
- Personal contact helps you get a permanent job. Is there an all-faculty potluck on a night you would rather stay home? Go! Who will be on the search committee if a position opens where you're an adjunct? Why, the faculty you've been chatting with in the copy room or over the pulled pork sandwiches at that potluck. The ability to demonstrate collegiality is an important factor in most hires.
- Students talk – about you and your teaching. Yes, they do – and you want it to be positive. I'm not talking about being "easy" so everyone likes you; that gets around negatively. I'm talking about being *good*. *So good, in fact, students tell everyone you are a fantastic teacher.*

GET READY TO LAUNCH

No Frazzle, Drama, Anxiety, oh My!

Getting Set Up As an Instructor

When you know about codes, where to go for IT help, budgets, copies, supplies, software available, etc., teaching preparation can be focused on developing lessons to maximize student learning and less on wondering how to "do" and "get." Many new instructors don't even know the right questions to ask until they've been hit with a problem. To help make your life easier from the start, here's a comprehensive checklist that should include almost all the vital information you need. Ask the questions. Having the answers in advance will make your life easier!

Your official supervisor is frequently a Dean of Instruction or perhaps a Department Chair. She or he may not be available very often, so ask to get a recommendation for a faculty contact in your field who can answer all the mundane questions (like who pays for ink in the communal printer). This way you'll get acquainted right away with other faculty and won't be a bother to your supervisor. Deans are busy people. Be sure to make friends with the department administrative assistants. They usually know everything and everybody and can be a tremendous help.

Important Names and Numbers

- ❏ Dean:_____
  - ° Office Phone:_____
- ❏ Faculty Chair:_____phone:_____
- ❏ Dept. Administrative Assistant:_____
  - ° Phone:_____
- ❏ Faculty "Mentor":_____
  - ° Office Phone:_____
  - ° Home/Cell Phone:_____
- ❏ College 800:_____
- ❏ Number to call if I can't make class: _____
- ❏ Switchboard:_____
- ❏ Maintenance contact:_____phone:_____
- ❏ Tech help contact:_____phone:_____
- ❏ Counseling Center for referrals:_____
- ❏ Student Services person handling cheating, etc. issues: _____
  phone:_____
- ❏ My phone number at college:_____
- ❏ College fax:_____
- ❏ My email here:_____
- ❏ Copy Shop number:_____
- ❏ Bookstore number:_____

Checklist of Questions to Get Answered

- ❏ Faculty handbook for me? On-line? Union contract/contact?
- ❏ All pay, retirement, and insurance paperwork filled out?
- ❏ In-services I should or could attend? Meeting requirements?
- ❏ Faculty photo ID? Faculty keys?
- ❏ Mailbox set up for me somewhere? When do I have access?
- ❏ Set up for eLearning Management System? Classes for it? Help numbers?
- ❏ When are my classes loaded? College policies for what must be uploaded (like syllabus or grade book)?
- ❏ Copy card or number? Access to copy room? Hours?
- ❏ Budget for copies?
- ❏ Computer to use? Printer? Scanner?
- ❏ Email account set up? Who does this?

- ❑ Computer access codes? Software programs available? Can I load test banks myself?
- ❑ Technology available in classrooms? Keys needed?
- ❑ How to get supplies? Pens/dry erase markers/etc. Budget?
- ❑ Policy on office hours?
- ❑ Locked place to put my files? Materials?
- ❑ Textbook and ancillaries order? Who orders? How? Due date for textbook orders? Do I choose them?
- ❑ Syllabus examples for me to look at for my courses?
- ❑ Do Common Course Outlines or goals for my courses exist?
- ❑ Can I alter curriculum? What goes into the change process?
- ❑ Writing, Math, etc. Resource Room tour/services? Hours?
- ❑ Library tour/services? Hours? Faculty library Card?
- ❑ Policies/help/info on student learning assessment?
- ❑ How to turn in grades? All online? Midterm required? Test required during Finals week?
- ❑ Any secretarial help available? Where? Who? Number?
- ❑ Student Services Personnel who help with troubled students?
- ❑ What is the faculty evaluation process?
- ❑ Whom do I turn to for help with teaching issues?
- ❑ Escort service for late night classes? Number:_____
- ❑ Emergency Plan for college? Where?
- ❑ What is the tenure process?
- ❑ Institutional or Program Core Goals to include in my classes?

Skill 1:

DESIGN THE CURRICULUM
What Content Do I Teach?

New teachers find themselves in a variety of situations from having all their courses handed to them already planned to the other extreme of having to prepare four classes from absolute scratch. Either way, designing a curriculum is an essential skill all college teachers have to develop eventually. Curriculum, assessment, and instructional strategies are all intertwined. You don't have a curriculum without a way to teach it (strategies) and assess whether or not students learned it.

More Than a Textbook

Many of us associate a college course with "moving from chapter one to chapter fourteen." We allow the textbook to *become* the course design. With a perfect text, matched perfectly to your audience, this may be OK to begin with, and certainly when you are hired a week before classes start, this is probably all you can do the first semester. But textbooks are developed for the "general" audience, not your particular set of needs. Unless they match your needs exactly, they should not define your curriculum design. Besides, you are the expert – students expect more from you than just a recitation of the text. After all, they can read books on their own.

Building Goals and Objectives

First, get over the jargon. Are they *goals*, are they *objectives*, or are they *outcomes*? Surely a dissertation or twenty has been written on this topic, but I am not trying to turn you into educational psychologists. Individual colleges and deans seem to ask for different language, so let's not get hung up here. Call them *whatevers,* but what matters is there are big guys and little guys involved here, and they define your curriculum.

START with Developing *Big Goals* for Your Course

Ask yourself: *"What broad topics/concepts do students need to know at the end?"*

Will you be introducing students to modes of essay development? To basic statistical concepts? To the Bill of Rights? To an understanding of the scientific method?

Goals are **broad statements** about what your course will cover/accomplish.

Goals are frequently (but not always) found in catalog course descriptions. They are so big they kind of define the course and differentiate it from others with similar titles (goals show the difference between Lifespan Psychology and Social Psychology). They are not always bullet-pointed out in the syllabus, but you may have the desire to do so.

Look at what others have set as goals for the same course. There is no need to re-invent the wheel when it is already round and rolling. Many college systems have Common Course Outlines (perhaps under a different name) that define course goals, and you cannot deviate from them. Holding goals in common helps assure all English Composition classes cover the same big items even with different teachers. You will want to locate the equivalent of a Common Course Outline for your classes. The Common Course Outline is college property. (Ask your Dean. These are usually published on-line.)

Your courses may fit into a program of study that counts on students acquiring certain knowledge bits and skills prior to taking advanced classes. What slice of this pie are your courses providing? A review of course goals with faculty who teach the upper level courses should help you see if their needs are being met. Very few courses stand completely alone; we are all interdependent to some degree.

You do need these "big guy" targets firmly in mind in order to set up the "little guy" targets: *objectives.*

Next - Develop Objectives or Learning Outcomes

Learning Objectives flesh out the broad goals.
Ask yourself: *"If students truly understand the scientific method (big goal) what is it that students will be able to do..."*

Objectives are the targets you aim for when planning your lessons, activities, and assessments.

Objectives are what the student leaves with – what they learned – what they are able to "do" themselves. *You will have several objectives for each broad course goal in order to cover it well.* If you have time, develop your own objectives for your course. Again, objectives may be dictated by your department, so ask first.

Good textbooks have objectives for every big goal. You can use or modify some of the objectives in the textbook, but weed through them for those that directly relate to your own course goals. Textbooks usually have way too many objectives for you to use them all. You can't have 87 objectives for a course and expect to cover them all.

Developing Good Objectives
- Good objectives relate directly to course goals
- Good objectives are clear and specific, not vague
- Good objectives focus on what <u>students</u> will do, not what the teachers will do
- Good objectives are measurable so you can actually test somehow to see if the students accomplished them

Here is a big course goal for a phlebotomy course: <u>*Students*</u> *become proficient at drawing blood.*

Here is a good objective that fits under the goal: **Students will be able to** *choose an appropriate phlebotomy technique, adapting to the health of veins.*

When developing objectives, ask yourself these questions:

IN the context of the goals set for the course,

What do students need to know about that goal when they walk out the door?
- What **knowledge bites** should they possess?

- ° *(What theories should every student who leaves an Intro Psychology class know? Which BIG names? Research findings on which topics?)*
- What **skills/procedures/processes** should they have developed?
  - ° *(Interpreting research data? Setting up a microscope? Critical thinking? Analyzing a research article? Inputting data into a statistical program?)*
- What **understandings**?
  - ° *(How parenting practices impact intelligence?)*
- What **attitudes**?
  - ° *(Healthy skepticism?)*

Come up with a few basic, salient objectives for each goal. When learned, together they should cover that goal at the appropriate level for your course. The trick? *You must be able to measure student success for each of your objectives.* If you have no way to really measure whether or not students have actually achieved the objective, then it is most likely too vague, too broad, or too lofty – or you just haven't figured out how to measure it yet. (How do you measure "healthy skepticism"? Some say you can't; I say keep reading. There are perception-based tools that may help in this instance.)

Make your objectives/outcomes realistic:
- An *introductory* course is foundational. It skims the surface. It doesn't need to teach or test on every concept in the field. What are the BIG ideas appropriate to the course level? Which do you have the actual time to cover adequately? Go for understanding of a few big concepts rather than flying through way too much information students will forget hours after the final exam.
- Upper division courses cover subjects in more depth. For these, you may want to find out what courses are prerequisites of yours and get their descriptions, goals, and objectives. This will show what you can expect students to have already learned, and you can develop your own objectives with this in mind.
- Objectives are always directly linked to how you assess and the strategies you choose to teach the content. If an objective says a student will be able to "demonstrate" something, then assessment should include some type of demonstration of that knowledge or skill, probably not a standard multiple-choice item. The activities you choose to help teach that objective should also engage students in "demonstrating." Curriculum, assessment, and strategies are always integrated.

Bloom's Taxonomy: Super Tool

When you are planning your objectives, semester activities, tests, and assignments you want to keep something in mind every K-12 teacher probably memorizes: Bloom's Taxonomy of Cognitive Levels. Education majors are very familiar with Bloom's Taxonomy and its tremendous usefulness, but for all those who aren't, here is a little history.

Way back in 1956, Benjamin S. Bloom, the Associate Director of the Board of Examinations of the University of Chicago, wanted to develop a way to classify statements of instructional objectives. He assembled measurement specialists from across the U.S. and they developed a hierarchy of levels for instructional objectives, published as *Taxonomy of Educational Objectives: The Classification of Educational Goals*. "Bloom's Taxonomy" was born.

There are three Bloom domains: *cognitive* (thinking, reasoning, remembering), *affective* (moods, feelings, attitudes), and *psychomotor* (movement, motor skills). The taxonomy for each arranges learning into a hierarchy based on complexity.

In 2001, Lorin Anderson and David R. Krathwohl, two people who had worked with Bloom, published a revision of the taxonomy developed by a group of educators (*A Taxonomy for Learning, Teaching and Assessing: A Revision of Bloom's Taxonomy of Educational Objectives*). The most notable change was a switch in position between evaluation (originally the highest level) and synthesis (creating – formerly the second highest level). The following table includes both versions.

Bloom's Taxonomy is a critical course design tool for everything from physics to modern jazz. While some classes (such as counseling, theatre, dance) may use two or even three domains, the bulk of college coursework focuses primarily on the cognitive domain – basically, *thinking* – so I will focus there too.

Faculty members frequently complain that students can't think. But what can they expect if they only ask students to memorize information and spit it back? That is the lowest level on Bloom's cognitive taxonomy: memorization of knowledge. If you want a different level of thinking you have to develop higher order objectives, ask different questions, and assign different projects to elicit that thinking.

Many instructors *assume* they are teaching and testing at the highest levels of thinking. Then they examine all their objectives and test items and feel shocked at how many sit at the two lowest levels of Bloom. You can easily avoid this situation with a planning grid. List out your current objectives, the assignments that help students demonstrate them, and test items that cover them. Then classify each for Bloom level. You can only change when you know exactly where you are to begin with. If you want students to develop and demonstrate evaluation skills you need an objective which focuses on evaluation, etc. You have to ask for it and plan assignments to build it!

Don't plan on eliminating Bloom's lower levels in all your objectives. That's going too far. The lowest levels are important prerequisites to the higher levels in any field. It is hard to become a creative chemist (synthesis) if you don't first memorize and understand molecular structure.

If you are completely unfamiliar with Bloom's Taxonomy, go to the web and look it up. There are many sites of tremendous benefit to you. They include lists and lists of words that will help you write objectives and test questions at each level of Bloom.

Bloom's Original Cognitive Domain Categories
(with my explanations)

Knowledge
- If your students have to "remember it" they are functioning at the knowledge level. They may have quite a variety of things to remember: facts, sequences, categories, theories, methods, criteria, etc. Don't underestimate this level's importance.

Comprehension
- This level requires more than regurgitation; it requires translation, extrapolation, understanding, being able to explain or summarize or paraphrase in their own words.

Application
- Students can take material they learned at the knowledge and comprehension level and apply it to a problem or a new situation.

Analysis
- Students can now take things apart, recognizing patterns, analyzing relationships, seeing connections, finding major elements, dissecting, distinguishing, relating assumptions, and recognizing relationships.

Synthesis
• This is the creative level. Students combine, integrate, etc. to develop something new: a pattern, a piece, structure, theory.

Evaluation
• The highest level where students are now evaluating, judging, appraising, etc. using standards and justifiable criteria.

Summary of 2001 Revised Taxonomy for the Cognitive Domain
(Anderson and Krathwohl, pp. 67-68)

Remembering: Retrieving, recognizing, and recalling relevant knowledge from long-term memory.

Understanding: Constructing meaning from oral, written, and graphic messages through interpreting, exemplifying, classifying, summarizing, inferring, comparing, and explaining.

Applying: Carrying out or using a procedure through executing or implementing.

Analyzing: Breaking material into constituent parts, determining how the parts relate to one another and to an overall structure or purpose through differentiating, organizing, and attributing.

Evaluating: Making judgments based on criteria and standards through checking and critiquing.

Creating: Putting elements together to form a coherent or functional whole; reorganizing elements into a new pattern or structure through generating, planning, or producing.

Skill 2:

MANAGE A COURSE PROFESSIONALLY

No Surprises = More Satisfaction

Students are happier when they know what they are going to learn, how the class will run, exactly what is expected of them, how assignments will be graded, how you are going to teach and communicate with them, and when everything is due. They hate it when instructors add or shift assignments during the term rather than plan everything out ahead of time. When students understand all requirements in advance and stay in the class you usually have a more committed group, less griping, and more satisfaction throughout the term.

So – if you don't want to sit in your office mumbling to yourself: *"Oh Lord, what am I going to do today?"* you need to plan ahead. Even if you only stay 2 days ahead with your own daily reading, grading and activities all semester long, it is darned important you get the skeleton of the semester defined and paced out ahead of time. After all, you have to pass out a syllabus on Day One and you have to choose textbooks in time for the bookstore to get them in.

Choosing Textbooks

Let's start here since the bookstore needs your order before the semester starts, plus a good textbook helps you with curriculum planning (Skill #1).

A good text certainly doesn't define a course curriculum, but one is still almost essential for an undergraduate class. First, find out if you even have a choice of books. Does the college want you to use a specific text? What are other teachers using for the same class? The bookstore may have already ordered before you were hired. So find out the lay of the land. If you do get to make choices, here are some suggestions to help you choose wisely:

- Get free instructor copies of different texts to peruse. The bookstore should be able to help you with reps' contact info. Also, ask some colleagues who teach (or taught) the same classes. What did they use? What do they recommend? Why?
- Compare the various texts if you have time to do so, but *order on time with the bookstore.*
- Look for currency of information, clear writing, and appealing visual format for our modern students who do not appreciate page after page of small print.
- Does the text match the emphasis and goals of your course?
- Are there objectives clearly detailed for each chapter?
- Are the objectives already aligned with Bloom for you?
- Can you use a lot of those objectives or refashion them?
- Are there multiple examples? Charts? Color? Tables? Histograms? Photos? These help explain difficult concepts.
- Are key terms pulled out and defined for students?
- Are there review questions for each chapter?
- Summaries of most important points by chapter?
- Are there critical thinking or application questions/sections?
- Are any current events/people pulled in to add value/interest?
- Is the reading level appropriate for your students? (Reading level can usually be checked officially in the campus teaching resource center.)
- What is the cost to students? Some books are ghastly expensive yet offer little more information than significantly less costly books. Is soft-cover available? On-line texts? Rental texts?
- What are the ancillary materials? Is PowerPoint available? Audio? Study guides? DVDs? Connected websites? Diagnostic tests? Etc. Just what is the package deal and who pays for it? Which ancillaries are free? Who gets to keep them – you?
- Will this one book work for you? Don't require multiple texts for a class if you plan on assigning only small parts of them. Students are resentful (and rightly so) when this happens.

The Syllabus

You need a syllabus for your class. Perhaps you were given one to use or perhaps you were given only a sample and you get to change it and make it your own. Either way, it has a function: to tell students on Day One what the class is all about.

The syllabus helps you develop that "no surprises" semester that provides a level of comfort for you and your students. Plan your syllabus carefully so you aren't passing out a revised version any time during the semester. The Common Course Outline (or equivalent) is college property, but the syllabus is your property. It is also sometimes seen as a "contract-like document" for teacher and students.

You should have a copy of your syllabus in paper form to discuss on the first day of the semester, and you should also post the syllabus to whatever eLearning Management System (LMS) your college uses. That may be a requirement – so check it out.

Syllabi appear in all sizes. There is the wimpy little one-page syllabus that gives students so little information about a class it is basically a waste of paper. Then, there is the 15-page budget eating version that includes color and graphics. When preparing a syllabus, *more* is generally better than *less,* but you can get too detailed. A really long syllabus, all in small print with very little white space, may offer "no surprises", but most students also don't read it. It's too visually overwhelming. Thus you end up with the same questions a wimpy syllabus gets: *"When is the first paper due?"* That's frustrating because the answer is clearly in the syllabus – on page 14. Surely, there is a happy medium.

A basic syllabus should be easy to read with sections clearly separated. There is talk in the field about making the syllabus far more student friendly and engaging with graphics and visuals and color. This is a personal decision. I may be a stick-in-the-mud, but I suggest putting far more time into planning the learning activities for class than into creating a jazzy "holy wow" syllabus.

There are at least 10 sections to be sure to include:

1.   Header:
Include full class title and ID number(s), number of credits, college you are teaching for, etc.

2.   Contact info:

Classic contact information so students can find you at the college and contact you various ways.

- Instructor's name. Phone number. Email.
- Class location. Class times.
- Office hours. Office location. E-office hours.
- Preferred method of contact.

You do need a private life too, you know, so be wise about giving out your cell phone number to undergraduates. With email and messaging inside surely all eLearning Management Systems these days, students can contact you easily anyway. If you give only your office number, be sure you know how to access that phone remotely if you don't come in every day. Students actually expect you are available and answering your phone Monday through Friday, normal hours. They get cranky when they can't get in contact with you.

The same courtesy applies to office hours. Put your office hours in the syllabus, with the room number, and then be there for the full time. If you must leave your office a small "I am in the building and will be right back" sign is a model of respecting others. You might also consider putting "e-office hours" in your syllabus and do a live chat on LMS to accommodate students who can't stop by your office during regular times. My colleagues who have done e-office chats at odd times when they would just be sitting at home reading or grading anyway have had good success with it.

3.   Description:

Usually instructors put in the course catalog description. Fine. You are probably required to use it. But those descriptions are sometimes pretty lean and boring. You might want to add a second paragraph to give your course some zip. Try to spice it up a little. What might intrigue students about the course content and its value to them?

4.   Course goals and/or objectives:

Follow the norm at your college. Some want broad goals only, directly copied from the Common Course Outline (or equivalent); others want both goals and objectives in the syllabus. There may also be a requirement for number of objectives per credit. All things to find out. (Remember, it is your syllabus and you can add in some objectives dear to your heart on top of any required ones.)

5.   Resources:

Please do list all the required texts and don't add anything mid-semester even if you found a new book you just love. Remember: no surprises. Clearly separate *Required* from *Recommended*. List your resources in the appropriate style for your field. If the bookstore doesn't stock some of your required items also give students information on where to buy them.

6.   Assignments:

In the syllabus give a good overview of each major assignment (like papers, projects, presentations, etc.). Choose your assignments carefully so each covers several learning objectives. Provide just enough information to give students an idea of what the course entails so they can decide to stay enrolled or drop. You can give specifics later, but mention you are going to do that.

7.   Evaluation system:

List what goes into computing the final grade (attendance, participation in class activities, lab reports, Paper One, Paper Two, midterm, final, etc.). Give the percentage or points allotted to each and the grading scale you will use. You might want to attach grading rubrics for major assignments or at the very least mention rubrics will be handed out well prior to the assignment's due date. With LMS available for all of us, it is easy to say inside the syllabus that all grading rubrics have already been loaded and are viewable on-line. That saves you some paper!

Check to see if your college or department strongly suggests using a certain grading scale before you invent your own.

Sample of Grading Information From a Syllabus		
You Will Be Graded On:	% of grade	Points
Five "five-paragraph" essays	25%	50
One ten page research paper	30%	60
In-class activities/discussion	20%	40
Peer Reviews	10%	20
Critical Thinking Journal	10%	20
Comprehensive Mind Map	5%	10

Grading Scale:

93-100%	A
86-92%	B
80-85%	C
75-79%	D
Below 75%	F

Grading Rubrics have already been uploaded for all graded projects and assignments – access them on-line.

Missed Class and Late Assignment Grading:
Attendance is expected, but there are no points for attendance. Instead, in-class activities will be turned in each class for points. In-class activities cannot be made up without a doctor or military excuse. Because I know "life happens," I will drop the four lowest scores from each student's in-class activities when I compute grades. Late work: Other assignments will be accepted for full points with a doctor or military excuse if turned in within one week of due date. Without an excuse, late assignments will be docked one grade per week past due date. Extenuating circumstances will be taken into consideration on a case-by-case basis, so contact me if you feel you fit into this category.

8. Policies and expectations:

Policies attempt to circumvent problems and warn students of consequences. For example: *Late papers will be docked 5 points for each day they are late. Papers will not be accepted if over 5 days late.* Policies have a tendency to morph a lot over time, usually as you get frustrated with something like tons of late work being turned in.

What defines a problem for one instructor won't necessarily be identical for another instructor. One person cares that people attend class. Someone else doesn't. One instructor won't accept any late work. Another doesn't care about due dates at all. One instructor can't stand cell phones in class; another has incorporated them into activities. One instructor doesn't care that students play solitaire or cruise Facebook on laptops they supposedly brought for taking notes. Other instructors hate this. These issues are quite individual, and because they are, they must be clearly communicated to students.

As you move through the weeks of class, jot notes about what policies you might want to change next semester. Remember, if you fail to say you expect people to show up to class each and every class in the syllabus and don't list the ramifications of skipping, it becomes very difficult to take points away from students when they disappear. They will protest. These are individual instructor decisions, but they have to be mindful ones.

DO NOT make such strict policies that you can't keep them and feel good about it. Frequently new teachers are too lenient the first semester, get annoyed, and become wildly strict, then realize they didn't leave any wiggle room for life events to happen to their good students. Eventually, they strike a happier balance between expectations and reality. The policies section will change for quite awhile as you grow as a teacher and find out what really annoys you and what isn't that important. Then it, too, will settle down into smooth flowing management.

It is good to reflect on whether or not a policy is really about your ego or about helping students learn. Err on the side of kindness and mercy. It's doubtful your course is near the center of the universe.

9.   Resources for Student Success

Your college may want you to include a statement about serving students with academic challenges or disabilities in each syllabus, telling them where to get the help they need (tutoring services, note takers, etc.). At most colleges there are pretty standard lines giving information about the Academic Success Center, "*if you need special accommodations….*" etc. You might also want to mention any program that offers help to students, like TRIO (they provide tutors for certain populations), as well as math and writing labs. Ask to see what is available at your school and help point students in the direction of success.

10.   Dispute Resolution for Grades and Academic Honesty

Provide a way students can resolve a dispute about a grade. One good way is this: "*It is your responsibility to retain all your graded material during the semester. If you disagree with any grade, do not address this through email. Set up an appointment with me and bring the graded material with you. I will be happy to discuss grading with you in person.*"

Also include a statement such as this one: *As for issues of academic honesty, consequences for plagiarism in this class, formal grade appeal process, etc., please read the XX college handbook on-line. This class will follow all XX guidelines and policies.*

If you want, quote the handbook on cheating and academic honesty and the very real consequences that can happen to any student who cheats and is caught. Students frequently do not define cheating the same way teachers do. If you do not want students to answer homework questions in groups, tell them you consider this cheating. Of course you don't want them to plagiarize, either, but please do not assume they even know what that means. You have to give specific examples. If you do not want them to cut and paste from Wikipedia or buy papers on-line at Cheaters.com and change a few sentences, be sure to tell them. Spell it out. Yes, it seems like we shouldn't have to, but we frequently need to. Some students have come from a very successful cheating career in high school. Other students come from cultures where working together for a goal would be considered completely appropriate behavior.

11. Because "Life Happens…"

You might consider adding this little section. It actually helps you out as much as the students. If you want to be judge and jury of every single little excuse for missing class (there are a LOT of them), with students begging to make up an activity, then skip this section. But if being judge and jury sounds like a real time waster and emotional bomb, then you'll want to consider this recommendation. It goes something like this:

There are 24 class periods in this semester. Each class will have an activity worth points. You cannot make up activities unless you have a written doctor or military excuse for your absence. However, I know that sometimes "life happens" so I will drop the lowest four activities when computing final grades. This way you could miss some classes and your grade will not be hurt. I will also drop the lowest two test scores.

This system saves students from making up lies or telling you too much about their personal lives. It saves you from having to sift through dramas attempting to tell which is really bad enough to allow a chance to make up work. This system also allows students to just have a bad day, which happens to all of us now and then.

Get Students to Read the Syllabus

How do you know students understand the syllabus? Seasoned teachers usually have students sign off to assure they have read and understood the syllabus. There are several ways to do this.

1. A simple form that says *I have read and understand the syllabus*
    Name_____ Date_____

2. More useful – Icebreaker Syllabus Scenarios in class plus the acknowledge-
    ment form. Make up several little scenarios which involve parts of the sylla-
    bus you want students to pay particular attention to.

    Mike has 12 points on Paper 1, 17 points on Paper 2, has never missed a
    class, but is two weeks late turning in Paper 3 because he went on a ski trip
    to Alaska. He didn't tell me until he got back. What will his accumulated
    grade be by midterm?

    Mary is disappointed that she got a "B" for the class because she received
    an "A" on all three papers and all the in-class activities that she did. Mary
    sets up an appointment with me and brings in all her graded work for the
    two of us to go over. We get out the attendance records and find that Mary
    missed seven classes. Did I make a math error or does the grade stand?

    Break students into small groups to answer. This gets students comfortable
    with classmates and helps them understand the syllabus. Five or six little
    scenarios provide a great group activity for about 10-15 minutes. If you can
    make humorous scenarios, so much the better. After you teach awhile, you
    can use examples from real life – there will be plenty!

3. Quiz over syllabus in the LMS (eLearning Management System). You can
    set up a single-item quiz which acts as an electronic signature or you can
    set up a several-question quiz over many aspects of the syllabus that must
    be completed until 100% correct before the student can move forward.
    Your LMS staff will help you if you don't know how to do this.

4. Expanded acknowledgement form. Same signature part, plus questions.
    Ask questions that might give you ideas for adding value to the class for
    students. If six students out of 35 in your entomology class are interested
    in non-chemical insect control you can group them deliberately for certain
    activities. Only ask questions if you hope to use the information to craft a
    better value for students.

Your major:_____Minor:_____
Two questions about this subject:_____
Interests, hobbies, or goals I have that this course
might touch upon_____

Semester Schedules

It is extremely helpful to include a detailed schedule of the semester with your syllabus, probably on a separate sheet. Hand it out and discuss it, but also put the schedule on-line.

Include the dates of each class, what students should do to prepare (read chapter 10, answer questions 1 - 7), the topic of the class, what is due (papers, projects), test dates, etc. Just double check all dates against the college academic calendar because you'll have to work around holidays, spring breaks, etc.

Date	Topic	Preparation	Due/Tests
Jan. 10	Basic Theories	Chap. 1	Questions 1 – 4
Jan. 17	Consciousness	Chap. 4	Questions 1 – 3, 7
Jan. 24	History of Psyc	Chap. 2	Questions 2, 5, 7, 9
			Test: Chaps 1, 2 & 4

Making changes to the schedule mid-semester is something to avoid. However, sometimes a class just isn't catching an important concept and you need to review, or there are snow days, sick days, and other life events that happen and you are the one who misses class. Always put this little phrase into the schedule somewhere: *The instructor reserves the right to alter this schedule to best serve the needs of students.*

Pacing a Semester and a Class

Learning to skillfully pace multiple classes over a semester happens with experience but why not prevent some of the trial and error pain involved at the beginning? It's a bit discouraging to run out of material three weeks before the semester is over but even worse to have six weeks of material left to cover and no time. Cramming is not productive for students or teachers. Here are some good pacing tips:

A semester planning table helps assure you cover all course objectives and all levels of Bloom's Taxonomy. You can easily see how this type of table helps an instructor spread out the workload appropriately for both students and themselves over a semester.

Planning Considerations	Week 1	Week 2	Week 3 ETC
Objectives to Cover & Bloom Level	Obj: Understand elements of introductions (Knowledge)	Obj: Recognize qualities of the good thesis statement (Comprehension)	
Preparation Homework Assignment (outside before class)	Read Chapter 2	• Read Chapter 3 • Bring three thesis statements you write to class	
Class Activity - ME	Lecture on Intro: multiple examples: model writing one from scratch	Lecture on Thesis Statements; model writing several on topics students suggest	
Class Activity- Students	Write one four sentence introduction; critique in groups using rubric criteria	Evaluate and rank six student samples (in groups of 6) – justify ranking (Evaluation)	
Grading &/or Feedback	Activity points	Activity points; feedback on thesis homework but not graded	

- Before finalizing your semester, put all class planning tables on your desk and see which weeks you gave yourself too much work to accomplish. Don't have major projects for all your classes due on the same day. You'll have a hard time performing a fast turnaround for students, and correcting too much at once impacts grading negatively. Spread out your own workload.
- Remember, all chapters are not created equal even in the best textbooks, so if you are planning "one week = one chapter" you might get stung. Some chapters can be combined; others will take several days of activities to help students truly understand a difficult concept. Look over your textbooks carefully and plan more by reading load and concept difficulty than by chapter.
- It's hard to pace classes themselves at the beginning. So always have backup activities on hand in case the ones you planned for the class take half as much time as expected. That happens. Then you and the students are sitting there

looking at each other. Awkward. Just make sure those backup activities involve critical thinking and are meaningful. Students know when you are "winging it" to fill a poorly planned class period.

- When you use small groups for your in-class activities, get ready for "group speed disparity." You will find some groups zoom through the activity and others dawdle. Now those dawdlers might be thinking the hardest or may be socializing instead of working. Walk around the class and join each group multiple times so you can help students learn to pace themselves. Give a "five minute warning" and "two minute warning" to get people focused. Keep an extension question on the topic ready to pass out to the speediest groups. This keeps them learning rather than discussing the weekend. An extra point or two will add motivation since many students do not consider more work a reward for getting done fast. Sweeten the pot.

Develop Class Patterns to Enhance Learning

Most good classes have a daily pattern or rhythm. You know what you are doing and students know what to expect. That doesn't make class boring; it makes class comfortable and secure. Without daily patterns, some students feel like every day may involve a new personal risk for them.

This is the pattern you do NOT want to fall into: students file in, sit down, you take student-by-student attendance (which takes too long), then you lecture with PowerPoint running for 50 minutes, you ask if anyone has any questions (no one does), then students leave. You do it all again tomorrow.

Three Example Patterns

Try to establish a pattern which engages students right at the start of class and gets them quickly into the material. Patterns should have a learning purpose. The pattern repeats every class (or week).

Example pattern 1:
- Start with students in groups.
- Have students answer one or two intriguing critical thinking questions involving the material they should have studied for class. Each student answers the questions by themselves FIRST on their scrap of paper and signs their name. Give 2-4 minutes. Students turn in their answers.
- The group then works together to discuss and craft the best answers.

- Have each group share their best response; make additions or corrections yourself so no erroneous information is being passed on.
- Watch your time. Allot perhaps 10-15 minutes tops.
- Then start your lecture on the topic, punctuated with application and extension of their answers and ideas, engaging students with the material every 10–15 minutes through a quick active learning strategy.
- Wrap up main points at the end in a quick summary and flash forward: *Today we covered four main points – 1, 2, 3, 4. Tomorrow we will see how this applies to X.*
- Remind them of homework due, projects coming up, etc.
- Dismiss class

Example pattern 2:
- Start with the whole class pondering a challenging question on the PowerPoint perhaps with multiple choice answers. Have them write down an individual answer.
- Have students turn to people around them and pair up with someone who chose a different answer. Have each person attempt to justify their answer, explaining what they based their decision on. Two minutes here.
- Stop the talk. Have students individually answer the question again.
- Reveal the answer. See how many have it right now. Discuss what threw them off and why the right answer is right. Clarify.
- Continue on into lecture + application. Have students turn something in during the activities so you get attendance without taking time for reading off each student name (boring).
- Wrap up main points at the end of class with a quick summary and flash forward.

Example pattern 3:
- Start out with a ten-question quiz, perhaps just matching or true/false. The quiz should be over the materials students were supposed to have read for class and should not be too challenging. (This helps them do their homework but doesn't stress them out every class period by having a hard test at the start.)
- Have them pass it in (there's attendance) and continue on with your lecture peppered every 15 minutes or so with application activities. OR if you choose, give them the answers to the quiz first and discuss any questions (keep track of your time here – be brief).
- Wrap up main points at the end of class with a quick summary and flash forward.

Patterns help students know how to prepare. Set them up with learning in mind. What do you want to make sure students do? Read the chapters? Apply the material to critical thinking? What patterns will help elicit that behavior? Think about having a daily pattern, plus a weekly or bi-weekly pattern. Quiz each week on the same day each time? Graded assignments always due on Fridays? Papers turned back the following Wednesday? Student presentations bi-weekly? Lab reports every Monday? Team meetings every Friday? When the same thing happens on a schedule, regularly spaced out, students are more prone to actually do their work. You are helping them learn to plan ahead.

A note on attendance: Federal Financial Aid requires faculty to be able to report the last day a student attended class if asked. This is for tracking and disbursing financial aid. You need to keep attendance records, but you don't have to do this by calling out each student's name at the beginning of class and taking several minutes to record. That is a pattern, yes, but it is one without a clear learning purpose for students.

Class-in-a-Box

As an instructor you will probably keep all your grades, assignments, etc. on-line in your college Learning Management System. Great. It is backed up daily and even if the whole system goes down you are unlikely to lose very much information.

However, just in case you don't have the luxury of a readily available LMS or for some reason you don't choose to use it, there is always the paper and file folder route.

For extreme organization the "Class-in-a-Box" system suggested here is outstanding. It is particularly useful for instructors who have to remain portable between multiple campuses and who grade by writing personal comments on paper. Even if you are teaching three different classes in three different buildings, the class-in-a-box system will keep you highly organized. No more lost papers and better teacher/student communication. Introduce this system on Day One and remind students about *returning their folders at the end of every class* for a few weeks until they fall into the pattern. Truly, this is a *great system*! You'll be super organized without much effort.

The basic Class-in-a-Box Pattern:

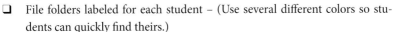

You'll need:
- ❏ A plastic box with a carrying handle for each class.
- ❏ Hanging files which hold syllabi, over-heads, pens, dry erase markers, tests, keys, roll lists, activities, etc.
- ❏ File folders labeled for each student – (Use several different colors so students can quickly find theirs.)

1. Students pick up their folders at the beginning of each class and put them in a stack *beside* the box at the end of class. You can quickly mark the unclaimed folders "absent." Presto. Role taken.
2. Establish penalties for taking the folder, like major point deductions. But don't knock points off the first few classes. Students have to learn the pattern of turning in their file folders as they leave class. You shape their behavior by reminding them regularly.
3. Staple a duplicate of your syllabus schedule into each folder or an abbreviation of it. Then due dates are a constant reminder.
4. When students need to turn in a paper or assignment, it goes into their folder. When groups do an activity and there is something individual to pass in, have students put it in their folder.
5. This is your communication system. Write notes to your students in their folders on little post-it notes. *"I'm worried about your attendance. Come see me." "You are really making some exceptional points in discussion. Great to have you in class."* Students can also leave you notes in their folders.
6. Pass everything back through the folders. It is private and students appreciate this.
7. Have students take home what you've graded; otherwise, the box gets too full and heavy. But always record grades before turning anything back in case someone leaves with their folder and loses it. This does happen quite often by accident as students are getting used to the system.
8. When you grade an assignment you may want to write the points earned on the schedule stapled inside the folder or have students do this. Students should never be in the dark about where they stand in your classes. You should also be putting grades on-line inside the LMS gradebook.
9. Keep your extra activity sheets, etc. in your box to pull out for formative assessment, when you experience group speed disparity, etc.

Checklist: Course Design and Management

- ❏ Check with department first about any goals required for your course(s).
- ❏ Check to see if any specific objectives are required or assumed.
- ❏ Find the Common Course Outline (or equivalent) for your course(s).
- ❏ Develop a few broad goals appropriate to the course level.
- ❏ Select the textbook carefully to match your goals and audience.
- ❏ Order the ancillaries (first find out who pays; will your budget cover these?).
- ❏ Develop specific objectives for each of your big goals, remembering more is not necessarily better. Use Bloom's Taxonomy.
- ❏ When writing objectives, take into consideration the knowledge, skills, procedures, processes, understandings, and attitudes students should have when they leave your class.
- ❏ Use a planning sheet to chart your presentation of objectives for the term.
- ❏ Design assignments and activities that correlate directly to your objectives.
- ❏ Make sure no assignment could be viewed as busy work, and that all are worth the time you expect students to invest in them.
- ❏ Plan a wide variety of ways to teach the material.
- ❏ Consider pacing of reading load and assignments. Allow students enough time to do a good job on projects. Allow yourself enough time to prepare and grade projects.
- ❏ Spread major points/projects throughout the term to avoid overloading students (and yourself) toward the end.
- ❏ Plan some type of assessment for all objectives so you know students have learned what you intend them to learn.
- ❏ Plan time for formative assessment. (More on this later.)
- ❏ Use Bloom's Taxonomy to make sure your activities, projects, and assessments go across several cognitive levels.
- ❏ Develop a clear, useful syllabus and a way to assure students read it.
- ❏ Develop a class daily pattern (or weekly, etc.) with a learning purpose.
- ❏ Create a semester schedule to give students with the syllabus.

Skill 3:

PLAN AHEAD FOR ACTIVE CLASSES

When students are truly active participants in class they learn more than when they zone out listening to instructors lecture on and on. Lecture is easy on students; they don't have to think or process the information. No one knows if they are even listening much less understanding.

If we want to maximize student learning we must make students active participants, busy with analyzing concepts, questioning, pondering, and thinking critically about how to apply those concepts out in their world.

Set the Stage for an Active Class

Day One is an important day. It sets a tone for the semester and it offers you the opportunity to build value for your class. If you can show students how this class will help them in 'real life' or their career or with future classes, you will indeed win them over.

Day One has several targets to achieve:
1. Let students know what the course is all about and what they'll be responsible for. Help align their expectations with reality.
2. Begin to learn student names.
3. Establish a friendly, professional, organized and safe atmosphere for learning.
4. Intrigue students with the subject material so they are excited about the class.

5. Get the class to begin working together so students experience an active learning environment.
6. Pretesting (if appropriate).

Several of these targets can overlap if you develop the right opening activity. There isn't any "right way" here; you will establish your own routine after experimenting.

Sample Day One

1. [Whole Class] Start off with a friendly introduction of yourself and why you are excited to teach this class, your qualifications, how you want students engaged and comfortable, the methods you'll be using to teach, etc., but keep this pretty short.
2. [Students in small groups or up and walking the classroom] Use an active icebreaker relevant to the subject matter to get students up and moving and meeting other students.
3. [Whole Class] Capitalize on the information in the icebreaker to intrigue students with the subject material. (more explanation of this later)
4. [Whole Class] Introduce and pass out the syllabus but do not read it word for word. Focus on critical parts like assignments, grading, policies.
5. [Students in small groups] Put students into groups to answer questions about the syllabus. Have them introduce themselves and tell something about themselves to their small group.
6. [Whole Class] Bring students back and answer questions about the syllabus and the class. Anticipate students may not feel like asking questions so have some to draw out of a hat and read/answer that you made up yourself. Help align student expectations with the reality of college level workloads.
7. [Whole Class] Have students either sign a document that says they received and understand the syllabus OR tell them they will need to take a short no points quiz over the syllabus on-line. (You want their signature or electronic record that they have received all your policies, etc. This helps avoid any problems later.)
8. [Whole Class with occasional Small Group Breakouts] At this point if the class has a lot more time, begin teaching. But be sure to include something very interactive for your students every 15 minutes or so.
9. [Whole Class] Wish students well. Give them the schedule. Remind them what is due for the next class. Mention all documents are on-line. Make sure you thank them for coming and emphasize you are looking forward to getting to know them and having a great semester together.

Use an Applied Icebreaker

I admit it! I was one of those students who HATED icebreakers because I felt they were a waste of time and I was shy. I'd go from class to class as an undergraduate and play that darned Name Game over and over, feeling extremely stressed about performing poorly. But not everyone is like me; I have since become an icebreaker convert. Some students absolutely need to meet others in order to feel comfortable in a class.

Icebreakers are a good way to loosen folks up and get them to bond. It's worth the time. Bonded classes who know each other's names function better and have better discussions!

Make sure your icebreaker applies to your subject matter not just to remembering names. There are books and websites listing hundreds of icebreaker activities because corporate trainers use them a lot. But these have to be adjusted to introduce the subject matter of your particular class. The size of your class also influences what you can try.

Important: don't do anything which causes anxiety or creates self-esteem risk. No "trust me" activities with blindfolds. Nothing "touchy-feely". Nothing where people have to touch one another's bodies in any way. (There are some really awful icebreakers!) Good icebreakers feel safe and they get people to talk and share, laugh and think a bit. Good icebreakers do not risk the self-esteem of introverted or shy students.

One successful icebreaker is Concept Bingo. It works like regular bingo except students use signatures not counters. Students are up walking around the room collecting signatures on bingo cards with questions instead of numbers. Loud background music helps eliminate any awkward silence.

The goal in building a good Concept Bingo game is to come up with statements students can relate to which cover concepts from the whole semester. In astronomy you might have questions like: *I've seen the Northern Lights,* or *I know where the North Star is.* In an ag class: *I've helped pull a calf; I know what a gilt is.*

In the Psychology Bingo example game shown here the statements cover all chapters in an Introduction to Psychology textbook. When a BINGO is reached and chocolate is passed out to the winner, the instructor goes over several of the questions in a humorous way: *"Only child, huh? What have we all heard about only children? That they are selfish, right? But we'll find out in chapter ten that isn't true at all! It's a myth!"* Each question gets a comment extending the simple item to a piece of research, attempting to provide value and interest students in psychology. This is a unique way of introducing an overview of the course and the many topics that interest psychologists. Students laugh, get to meet classmates, and get an introduction to the course.

Student Instructions: Psychology Bingo

Circulate. Walk. Talk. And ask each other questions. Find a student who fits the description in the box, share names, talk with them about "their square", and have them sign their name. Students can't sign more than one box for each person. Five squares signed in a row (any direction), yell BINGO! There are prizes!!

B	I	N	G	O
Knows someone who suffered brain trauma	Is a single Mom or Dad	Has had at least six different jobs	Has a grandparent over 85	Has been known to meditate
Is an only child	Has taken the Myers Briggs Personality Inventory	Speaks more than one language	Has trained a dog to do something amazing	Has an awesome memory for sports trivia
Knows what Roy G. Biv stands for	Has been hypnotized	Takes notes in color	Knows someone with narcolepsy	Was born prematurely
Gets 8 hours of sleep most nights	Was very shy as a child	"Went along with the group" sometime when you shouldn't have	Has driven past their driveway because they were thinking too hard	Thinks he/she is an introvert
Has a cat that runs to the kitchen at the sound of the can opener	Knows someone with PTSD	Can multitask	Has been able to break a bad habit	Is a really laid back, mellow person

Use/Learn student names

Really put effort into learning student names as rapidly as possible. On Day One you can start the process by asking students to introduce themselves to each other when they are put into small groups for an activity. Then when the class gets back together have a volunteer from each group introduce the group members to the whole class. If you have a small class, pass out a drawing of your room and have students sign where they are sitting. You can refer to this sheet while conducting discussions or asking questions. (Make the drawing large enough to be useful.) Tell students you are using it to learn names because you want to learn them quickly. Always say "hi" to students when you see them outside class.

Pretest

Pretesting is very appropriate in some classes (especially math) where prior knowledge is essential. It is a common activity on Day One. What you do with the results will vary between recommending a different section to some students (always a private discussion), to holding a "catch up" class not everyone is required to attend, to providing background handouts to fill in the knowledge gaps, to just quickly reviewing the key prerequisite concepts for the first week.

Align Student Expectations with Reality

Students (especially those coming straight from high school) have expectations about college that may be quite a bit off base. They may think everyone will be the same age, it's party time all the time, class is optional, professors all lecture, etc. Expectations shape behavior. And expectations themselves are shaped by prior experience. Their prior experience includes K-12 practices and media messages about the college environment. You may want to have small groups talk about their expectations and see if they are on track to understand the many differences between high school (example: where extra credit is the norm) and college (where it is unusual). Potential areas to discuss:

- classmates
- classrooms (size of classes, etc.)
- technology
- reading skill necessary for the texts
- study guides
- tests
- homework

- note taking
- teacher's role
- teacher attention and help
- types of instructional strategies that will be used
- deadlines
- points for effort

- extra credit
- amount of studying
- group projects
- grading and feedback
- what participation means
- behaviors expected in class
- consequences for academic dishonesty

Keep Lectures Lively and Students Actively Learning

Students nodding off in class? You do not have to be a clown or juggle piglets to keep student attention. Instead, you need to master presenting a lecture interrupted frequently with students applying the concepts you just covered. It's pretty easy to do. We just need to plan ahead and design active classes.

Lab classes are not the problem. Any lab class usually keeps students interested and learning. Why? Because they are doing something. They are moving. Talking. Figuring things out. In lecture classrooms, however, we easily notice the disengaged – the sleepers, yawners, texters. Adding active learning strategies will help them all be engaged.

Many college instructors think a lot about their content/curriculum and not enough about how *exactly* they will help students remember/learn that content. But planning for student learning makes the difference between TEACHING and simply PRESENTING information. You have to spend significant energy planning instruction if you want to be superior at teaching.

Active Learning – The Philosophy and the Drawbacks

The Philosophy:
For way too many years, college education has involved students primarily as passive learners/listeners. Lecture worked well for a minority of students, but it left many others struggling and bored. Now that we know so much more about the brain, information processing, memory, and learning, we have other, better ways to reach students. We know the more actively students are engaged with information the more likely they are to understand and retain. This doesn't mean they have to be physically active, up running around, but they do have to be mentally active. *Listening* is not mentally active enough for the majority of people.

Active learning shifts the focus from the teacher – *"I am the Great Amazing Lecturer"* – over to the students: *"How much are they actually learning?"* It requires we rethink how we present content so students get to do something meaningful with it, *right now.*

The Drawbacks:

- Many students still expect lectures as the primary mode of information transmittal in the college environment. They will be resistant. Don't drop all lecture from content-rich courses. That is not a good idea. Lecture + activity is a better combination.

- Some teachers are personally resistant. Lecturing is actually easier in a way once you have a set of notes you can repeat over and over. Lecture offers more control over the classroom. It's comfortable. The problem is it just isn't the best way to teach and actually have students learn.

- Students may have experienced only low-level simple activities under the guise of active learning. This turns everyone off. As one university professor said: *"There will be no small group work in this literature class. Why would I want the blind leading the blind?"* Ouch. Not much respect for student brains and insights. But there are two points in here. First, you are not the only person with knowledge and accomplishments in the room. Others have much to contribute. Second, you have to craft good questions to challenge students and have a way to out-process so no erroneous information is passed on. Then those small groups accomplish something – learning! There are ways to do this!

- Active learning techniques are easy to find all over the internet. But those used in corporate environments may not work well in college. Corporate training happens in brief spurts, not over an entire semester. Use corporate resources for ideas, but be willing to modify the activities.

Activity Variety and Learning Styles

There's a lot of research and writing, pro and con, on the topic of learning styles. Proponents say students have a certain preferred learning style (usually classified as visual, auditory, or kinesthetic) and learn best when presented information in that style. Skeptics say research doesn't support big learning differences if students are or aren't taught in their preferred VAK learning style.

But VAK learning styles aren't the only ones in the literature; they are just the most discussed in the U.S. What about Concrete/Abstract, Reflective/Active, Solitary/Social, Theorist/Pragmatist? And it goes on. EEkk! How do you juggle all this? You don't.

Plan ahead to use a wide variety of active strategies and you won't have to worry about learning styles. With variety embedded in lectures, activities, and assignments, you are fully covered. Don't always use pairs to answer questions; mix it up with people working alone, people working in groups, etc. Ask concrete questions. Ask abstract questions. Pose theoretical problems; follow up with application. This is basically sound teaching.

Important: it is *not* considered variety to stand and talk (auditory) about a PowerPoint (visual) while students take notes (kinesthetic). Too much of this can be a bloody bore.

YES, You Can LECTURE! Dynamic Direct Instruction

Lecture has been given a bad rap. Students want a certain amount of lecture – just not ALL lectures. A good lecture from a motivating, expert instructor is a fantastic *beginning* to learning if it includes time for application/analysis/etc. from students.

Get to class a few minutes early and write your agenda on the board. As you finish each item, check it off. This helps keep you and students on track.

> **TODAY**
> ❑ Review of classical conditioning components
> ❑ Preview
> ❑ Introduction to operant conditioning
> ❑ Break
> ❑ Activity on operant conditioning
> ❑ Review activity
> ❑ Quiz

1. **Review.** Start with a little review to place students in the context of what has come before. Example: "Yesterday we left off with classical conditioning… drooling dogs. You will remember classical conditioning is a basic type of learning involving….blah blah blah." (Hit highlights for 3 minutes, don't review the whole lesson.)

2. **Preview.** "Today we are going to look at operant conditioning and how these two types of learning are different and similar…" Show the objective(s) for the day, which will be right out of your syllabus. *After today, you should be able to…. 1, 2, 3, 4.*"

3. **Lecture.** Provide no more than 15-20 minutes of highly organized lecture material at a time. Interested adults can only focus for about 20 minutes at the tip top, and then their minds start to wander. This focus time may be getting shorter. The younger the class, the shorter their focus span it seems, so adjust accordingly.

    a. Define the concept. Give prototype examples students can relate to.

    b. Tie new information in to previously learned concepts. Point out the connections.

    c. Use visuals like charts and graphs.

    d. Give multiple examples. Use student majors/interests in your examples if at all possible. Use real life examples students are familiar with.

    e. Foreshadow connections to what will be coming, if appropriate.

4. **Stop and engage**. After the brief lecture, engage students in a review of the information you just gave. Use one of the active techniques listed later in this book that doesn't require too much movement, like Pair-Share, or Clicker Questions. This is a brief segment to make sure the harder concepts or terms have been explained well. *"First explain to your partner what an unconditioned stimulus is in your own words. Then look at the handout to make sure you are right. Partner, give a simple example of an unconditioned stimulus in a real life situation."*

5. **Ask questions.** Ascertain if students understand. Don't ask *"Are there any questions?"* yet. Instead, ask tailored questions to get at certain points in the material: *"What are two differences you see in operant conditioning and classical conditioning?"* Have students huddle in pairs or triads to come up with an answer.

6. **Active Practice.** Have students actively practice what you just taught in a meaningful, challenging activity in small groups. Example: *"Using operant conditioning plan a program to train a dolphin to jump through a hoop. Bullet-point the steps and use correct terms. Take about 5 minutes."* Have students sign their names to their sheet of paper and turn it in. (This is your attendance and having to pass it in with names also spurs a little more effort.)

7. **Process.** Go over the activity as a whole class now. Ask a couple groups to share. Ask probing questions: *"Why did you choose that schedule of reinforcement at the beginning?"* Give feedback. Wrap up the topic.

8. **Lecture.** Start over at #3 with the next major objective, tying it to what you just did, or review if you feel more is needed.

KEY: The combination of lecture and activity maintains motivation for most students and facilitates learning and remembering.

TIME issues – You will get better and better at monitoring time as you teach. You should be able to get through two cycles of this punctuated lecture during a 50-minute period eventually. At the start, you'll probably get through one. That's OK. They will have learned the concepts.

The Value of Images, Stories, and Fun

Our brains love to process images. Think about how much available information is contained in a single snapshot image versus how many words you would have to write out to fully describe the same scene. Images help us process and help us remember. We've been using our brains to process images a lot longer than we've been using them to process the written word. You can use our innate talent for remembering images to help students learn and remember.

Using Images as you Lecture:
- As you walk through a theory or concept, illustrate it with visual images, even those you sketch out yourself. Stick figures and arrows work just fine. Almost all classrooms have some sort of projection equipment for paper/pen.
- PowerPoint might be clean, versatile, techie, and used everywhere – but instructors who can draw cartoon figures and images to illustrate a lecture *as it unfolds* may capture the attention of students far better because they do not know what is coming up next. It draws attention.
- Eventually, have individuals or groups develop images that explain a concept or theory and present it to the class.
- Emphasize the importance of including their own hand drawn images in outlines and notes.
- Imagery research supports this technique – use of images may not only improve immediate recall, but long-term retention as well. (Caskey and Meier).

Using Stories:
- Stories are auditory images…the storyteller paints the images with words and we complete them in our brain. A really well-told story can be an effective way to help students remember.

- Not everyone is a storyteller. If you have no natural tendencies in this direction, don't go here without a lot of practice. You don't want to put your class to sleep. But most of us have stories from the trenches we can share to emphasize pieces of content. Students love well-told war stories when they directly apply to content.
- Use stories from the news if you find ones targeted to your learning objectives.

Using Games (especially to review for a test):
- Games with a point are fun – they take some of the seriousness out of class and this can be a good thing. If they aren't going to improve learning, however, don't use them!
- Jeopardy is a popular review game. The free template with clapping and music you can download from the web works very well and is easy to modify for any subject area.
- You can have students develop the Jeopardy panels – you don't have to do it all every time. Groups can administer their panel to the rest of the class.
- You can work to convert almost any TV game show for test review.
- Point basketball (complete with hoop) adds a physical dimension. Each group draws a question – if they can answer it correctly in 20 seconds they get to throw the ball for 2 points. The highest scoring team at the end gets something… food, drinks, or extra credit points.
- Games set up competitiveness – but this is very different than the atmosphere of a competitive classroom. Review game competition rarely backfires. Instead, there is usually lots of laughter, good-natured ribbing, and higher test scores for some students. (A competitive classroom is demotivating to many students.)

Qualities of Good Active Learning Activities

When you design active classes you will need to create good activities with the following qualities:

Your best activities
- ❑ Directly relate to the lesson objectives at hand
- ❑ Require critical thinking to complete
- ❑ Are enjoyable and interesting, not silly or childish
- ❑ Add real understanding and value (rather than take up time)
- ❑ Can be finished within the class period

❑ Can be "out processed" within the class period so students have feedback about the correct answers (not always possible)

❑ Provide variety – you don't use the same activity too often.

Follow these suggestions, and you will truly be able to design active classes that help students stay attentive and learn.

Skill 4:

IMPLEMENT ACTIVE LEARNING TECHNIQUES

From nursing to civil engineering, English to automotive, almost all teachers have some lecture classes. I have yet to hear a teacher say their students are fascinated and focused for these 50-minute to 3-hour lectures, either. I do hear teachers worry about having "too much content" to use activities. I feel this is shortsighted. *Giving* the content doesn't mean students are *learning* the content. The Content Dump approach only makes us feel we are doing our jobs (until the next test results come in).

10 FAST TRACK Active Learning Techniques (2-5 minutes)

The most content rich class in the world can pause three times during a 50-minute period and devote 2-3 minutes to getting students actively engaged. Students will learn more. There are dozens, perhaps hundreds of sites on the internet that give suggestions for quick learning activities. My thanks to all the universities, teachers, and trainers who provide such a rich service. (Many resources listed in the back.) The activities here are not all new, but the oldies have been tweaked to better fit a semester-long lecture class.

These Fast Track techniques are very brief. Introduce them quickly. Instructions on the PowerPoint help. The first time you do any of these, you'll startle a lot of folks who have been thinking about how they are going to spend Friday evening, so you might give a little more time to complete. But after that, stick to your time limit. You'll get used to being a Time Drill Sergeant. Students will start to catch on and get to business faster. If you use these activities consistently and follow them up randomly with a written product to turn in for points, students will pay more attention to your lectures.

1. Pair Share – With Different Applications

- Ap 1. Stop your lecture and ask students to pair up and explain a concept to a partner as if their grade depended on it (understanding) and give an example from their own life (application). In psychology an example would be (right after explaining this yourself), *explain the difference between a schema and a script to your partner and then give an example of each from your own life.*

○ An extension of this is to have each student write down the example his/her partner gave and explain (in writing) why it is a schema or a script. Pass in. Give points for a good job. Attendance taken.

- Ap 2. Quick partner up and answer this question. (You provide the question; make it challenging.) You can also have different questions for different parts of the room. Ask one or two pairs to answer for each question. Correct or extend and on into your lecture you go.

- Ap 3. Have students write down a question on the material they know the answer to. (They need scrap paper.) Put the answer on the back. Pass it to the right. Pass again. Again. Now students answer the question they hold. Pair with a close person and switch questions. Answer. Double check with each other and make sure answers are right. Spot check for accuracy.

Switch student partners occasionally: *turn to the person behind you…to the left…* This develops some low level peer pressure to process information attentively and gets students to meet new people and hear new views.

2.   Clicker Questions (and the colored paper equivalent)

Clickers (if you are not acquainted with them yet) look a bit like a TV remote. They work wirelessly with software on your computer and students can answer a variety of questions or polls with them. When used well, they help keep students actively engaged. Students answer and (if your technology is being co-operative) you see all the class answers on the PowerPoint.

- If you have access to a set of clickers from your department, you can use them easily to punctuate your lectures.

- If you don't have clickers available, go low tech. Remember, great teachers did exist before technology. If each student is given four squares of colored paper with A, B, C, D written on them you can easily use this technique. (Cheap Oriental Trading Company dry erase paddles and markers work great too.)

- Throw a multi-choice question up on PowerPoint or the board. Have students answer it either with clickers or by holding their paper squares/paddles up. You can tell at a glance how many people have the right answer. You can stop there and clarify (short version) – but a better idea is to have them turn to a partner and each explain why they chose that answer. Then let the whole class vote again. Did more people get the right answer, or are there lots of misconceptions out there? Have students explain why they changed or didn't. Then you can weigh in with the correct answer, and let students who had it right explain it. (This iteration makes the exercise longer but also more engaging.)

Clickers can really be over-used and become annoying rather than useful, especially in classes where instructors use mainly the opinion polling option. Clickers are good tools, but stretch yourself to use them with a learning goal in mind.

3.   Instant Memory Technique

* Stop your lecture and have students form pairs or triads and develop a technique for remembering the concept(s) you just covered. Students will usually work out a memory technique that requires them to understand the material. Have students share their techniques and they will be helping everyone in the class learn the concept. You'll also be able to catch misunderstandings and correct them.

4.   Similes/Analogies/Metaphors (with Words and Drawings)

* A simile: Active learning is like gymnastics practice. An analogy: He is swimming upstream with that business. Metaphor: My office is a fish bowl. Stop lectures and request students build a simile, analogy, or metaphor for a concept. Then have a few pairs explain their answers. Ask students to silently evaluate their own answer and see if it really explains the concept. This works well as a group, pair, or individual effort.
* You can ask people to draw their simile, etc. and explain it.

5.   What's Wrong With This Yell-Out…or…Make This Right!

* Interrupt your lecture with a projection of an image, statement, etc. but something with a *real error* in it. This is, of course, on the material you just covered. Invite anyone to Yell Out what's wrong. Keep asking until someone has the right answer. This is fun and useful because as you begin to test students and see what they actually become confused with, you get a lot of material for items. That means each semester you teach the same class you can help students avoid common misunderstandings with this little technique. (You can have students write their answers down first and have them turned in too.)

6.   PreCheat/Post Testing

* OK, this doesn't sound like an active learning technique, but it sure can be. Develop a few test questions over the material you will cover. This test can be True/False or other quick formats, but a fill-in-the-blank format works really well. Put it on PowerPoint or have paper copies (my preference). Have students take 2 minutes before you start the lecture to write answers. They can walk around and get answers from other students if they aren't

sure of something. 'Consultation' is definitely allowed here. Then start your lecture. When you are ready to break, have students individually (or in pairs) answer the Post test you are presenting. The questions here should include main points from the Pre test as well as application. Passed in, this gives you both attendance and a very good idea if students are connecting with the material. Don't make either test too long.

7.   Next Step? First Step? Last Step? Why?

- Perhaps the title is self-explanatory. You introduce a process, like writing code, diagnosing a patient, or a car with a problem. You take it just so far and then ask the question: *Next step? Why?* Any configuration of solo, pairs, small groups, etc. will work. Give a minute to write down the answer, and then process.

8.   Multiple Colors Question Bowl

- This is a great activity to help develop deeper thinking about a topic during an entire lecture. You start by writing several questions over the first 1/3 or so of your lecture at the knowledge or comprehension level. Then another set at the application or analysis level. Then the last set at the top of Bloom's taxonomy, the evaluation or synthesis level. The later questions build off answers to the earlier questions. (Use your test bank for help.)
- Copy each set of questions on a different color paper. Cut them up as little strips and fold them all into a bowl/box/tray of some sort. Put the containers around the room for every 3 (or so) students.
- How you structure the number of questions is up to you. You may want each bowl to contain the same questions, or each bowl to contain different questions.
- During the lecture *pause* when you know you have covered the material for Color 1. *"Get into small groups and pull a yellow question out. Answer it to everyone's satisfaction in your group. 20 seconds."* You will want to process the answers for accuracy, and then move on to another yellow question or back to lecture.
- When you are through with the next part of the lecture, on to a different colored question set. *"This time choose the two white questions. 1 minute to answer."* The second set of questions will require more time because they are more involved at the analysis and application level. It will also take a little more time to process as a whole class.
- You get the idea – on to the next lecture section and the next color. The last question set should really stretch students to think critically and recall and incorporate the information they learned along the way.
- Total time? Maybe 10-15 minutes for 3 question sets. Really worth your time.

9.   Three Do's, Three Don'ts (or two or one) Why?

As the name says, you present information and the students then generate three Do's and three Don'ts (which you have brought up while discussing the topic). Alone, this leans toward the knowledge end of Bloom's taxonomy. Paired with the *Why*, students have to display comprehension and more.

10.   IF AT [*] (Immediate Feedback Assessment Technique Scratch Offs) for Test Type Items

• Epstein Educational Enterprises, Inc. makes the IF AT, which looks somewhat like a lottery scratch off game for tests. It makes a nifty group activity. The scratch offs have 4 possible responses per item, 25 items to a card. The correct answer has a star under the scratch off covering so students get immediate feedback. No star, oops, we have the wrong answer. Think harder and try again. Some instructors give 3 points for an immediate 'star', 2 points for 2 tries, 1 point for 3 tries. Many types of activities work with the IF AT. If you can write multiple potential answers to a question, the IF AT will work. The sheets are a bit pricey so cut them up. One sheet will serve 5 groups if your activity uses 5 questions. That makes the cost well worth the expenditure. Just realize that when you divide sheets up you also have to reorder questions so answers match the key. IF AT sheets come with answer keys and I believe at this writing they have three different response sets. If you use IF ATs a lot you don't want students to figure out that #2 is always 'A' so get a few of each different set and mix things up. Students really enjoy IF ATs. If your budget allows give pairs a single sheet and include questions all the way through your lecture for them to answer together. There are many ways to use this low tech tool.

Backup Multipurpose Activities

Develop some general active learning activities that can easily be used with a variety of subjects and concepts on the spur of the moment. You may want to make copies, 4 to a sheet, cut them up, and keep them handy to use when something else doesn't work or the class flew through your material. I always carry a couple with me into any class. Their usefulness is pretty obvious. You verbalize the concepts, time periods, theories, etc., and students answer the questions. These work with groups or pairs, but done individually, they are also powerful assessments of the current level of student understanding. All take critical thinking. Time: 2–10 minutes.

Topic: ___[nuclear energy]_____[feedlots]_____	
PROS	CONS

Compare:___[civil war] _____with _____[revolution]_____	
Similarities	Differences

Question:_____[How to stop soil erosion in desert terrains]___	
Brainstorm multiple solutions 1. 2. 3. [several slots here]	Choose the one best, explain why

2 actions: _____[x]____and ___[y]_____	
Which is Most economical? Most ethical? Most feasible?	Why?

Topic:_____[day care for infants]_____
Which variables impact the outcomes?

In any subject area you will find designing fast track activities for solos, pairs, and small groups a pretty easy task. Why? Because many of the ideas flow from questions you wish students were asking themselves.

Here is a list of questions/suggestions to help start your own invention of lecture interruptions.

What are we assuming? Should we?

Why is this the right solution? The wrong solution?

How would you start? Why there?

What kinds of questions should we be asking now?

Give me an example of….

How does this connect back to 'X'?

How would you apply this in… (life, war journalism, geriatric practice, etc.)?

Summarize the 3 most important points.

What information are we missing?

We have a lot of data. Which is the most important?

What's the most basic concept we need to understand to solve this?

Restate in your own words.

If this problem goes unsolved, what are the potential complications? Why?

Which is best for…(x)?

Which concept applies here? Why?

What do we need to measure?

What are the potential effects?

Are there some alternative ways of handling this?

Are there some alternative conclusions to consider?

What information are we missing?

Draw the process.

What could happen next? How do you know?

MEDIUM LENGTH Active Learning Techniques (10-30 minutes)

"Apply-sheets" and Scenarios

"Worksheets" have an awful stigma, so call them something else, but when you generate your own "apply-sheets" [Ap-S] for a specific topic covered in your 15-20 minute interactive lecture, they are excellent active learning tools. You can design these as scenarios or case studies too. You need to plan ahead and copy ahead. Make sure you focus directly on the objective at hand, giving students a chance to immediately apply what they just learned. The primary cognitive levels here are usually analysis and application, so of course students have to know and understand the information first. Don't emphasize rote memorization. Go higher. You want students discussing and wrestling with the information.

Lecture ➔ Apply-sheet in Groups ➔ Out-processing ➔ Back to Lecture

Examples from a psychology class:

Example You have just covered Kohlberg's Stages of Moral Reasoning

Ap - S: You pass out a real Kohlbergian Dilemma used in research studies. Students must solve the dilemma in a small group for each level of moral reasoning.

Example You have just covered classical conditioning.

Ap - S: You pass out a scenario about a student who has high test anxiety. Students must work through the elements to identify the classical conditioning components and give suggestions for extinguishing the behavior.

Example You have just covered the information processing model of memory.

Ap - S: You give students a list of sensations, memories, and thoughts to place into the right section of the information processing model.

Benefits: You can make your own "small bite" apply-sheets and scenarios that relate right to your current lesson/objective. Students love applying information immediately, which solidifies their understanding and illuminates their misconceptions. Great group interaction too! Plus you have something in your hand with names on it for attendance and assessment.

Constructing

When you had to build a model of soil erosion with real water and real dirt in elementary school, your teacher was on to something, and you probably remember the principles of soil erosion to this day. We can use the building technique extremely effectively in the college environment as well. Here are some suggestions:

Building processes with human bodies

Whole classes can act out a complex process. One of the best examples of this is a demonstration of how information gets from one computer to another over the internet. The technical college faculty member we saw use this technique comes prepared with big bold signs for each stage of the process, which students can hang around their necks. While explaining the process, as he adds the next component, he adds a student to the living model. Eventually, the room is connected with students holding a rope between components. Then student volunteers can verbally (and literally) "walk" through the process. Or a round robin can take place with the first student in line saying what they do and the second student taking the "message" from there. This has been very effective and is a good example of using a "build it" active learning technique. It combines visual, auditory, and kinesthetic learning.

Building processes with slips of paper

Many types of processes can be modeled with simple slips of paper. At first you might need to provide slips of paper with each stage of the process already written down. Then groups of students put them into the right order. Other groups can circulate around and see differences. Discuss any differences and make sure the right sequence is identified. Eventually, you might have student groups come up with the stages of the process themselves. They can create slips of paper for each step and then groups can switch and attempt to put together each other's process. This can lead to excellent discussion about what is necessary and what happens when processes are out of order or missing components.

Building models

You can engage students in building models in groups. Anatomy is a subject area that seems to be straight boring memorization in so many classes, but it doesn't have to be. Playdough to the rescue! After the anatomy instructor goes over the components of the knee, student groups can "build" a knee out of playdough and put toothpicks in the component parts. Then groups can rotate and identify each part marked by the toothpicks. The act of shaping the parts with your own hands is quite different than just looking at a picture or even handling an expensive plastic model. Physical modeling, of course, will work well for a variety of classes. Put a time limit on construction to keep the class moving.

Reconstructing

Some subject areas, like English composition, lend themselves to the activity of reconstruction. To demonstrate how coherence works to develop "flow" in a paragraph, give students paragraphs cut up by sentence. A well-written paragraph should be able to be *reconstructed* because of tight coherence. Pairs attempt to reconstruct the paragraph, discussing why they put it in the order they did. Several different samples illustrate different methods of developing coherence. To apply this personally, have students cut up their own paragraphs to see if classmates can reconstruct them. Invariably students have trouble putting one another's initial paragraphs back together in the "correct" order. A lot of discussion erupts about this failure. Students get the chance to revise their work, cut it up again, and repeat. Classes learn what coherence is because they need to revise their work until other students can reconstruct their paragraphs consistently.

Students generally find this a lot of fun. They take it as a challenge to write so clearly that anyone can reconstruct their paragraphs. You can "reconstruct" in other content areas too.

Gallery Walk

Almost anything groups of students put together or draw out on paper can be turned into a Gallery Walk, which taps into the cognitive level of evaluation. Put the student work out around the room. Large paper hanging on walls is my favorite way to do a gallery walk. Have small groups rotate on your signal to each station. With a specific set of questions to answer students will be guided into careful attention to detail, analysis, etc. Questions depend upon the project and the objective you were striving to cover. Don't give groups too much time at each station so they have to stay focused. Let them end with their own work and see if there are now some things they would change. Out-process. Having each student take notes on each project (to turn in) helps most stay focused.

LONGER Active Learning Techniques – Larger group techniques/ more time

You, of course, can come up with numerous ideas on your own for activities that will take the better part of a class and keep students involved. This is the domain of the case study or the direct application of multiple variables (and multiple objectives) in your field. Longer activities include problem-based learning and the unfolding case study.

Many fields (like nursing) have examples of longer evidence-based best practices for teaching available on-line. No need to reinvent what works, so look for active learning techniques within your own field. Just one suggestion: you can lecture for 20 minutes, have students start a case study and answer the first few questions (you covered that info), then lecture again, break to continue, etc. Here are just a few examples of instructor-designed longer learning activities:

- Design a double-blind research study to get at XXX under these parameters…
- Review the case study of the patient and revise protocols the nursing staff can use for a better outcome.
- Using what research tells us about early childhood daycare, design a state-of-the-art daycare facility incorporating the science of development.
- Take this website and, in pairs, revise it optimally to maximize SEO.

- Take this brochure and analyze it for marketing appeal to a younger audience. Make recommendations for change.
- Write an "instruction manual" for a procedure. Have others try it out.

There are other, general types of longer active learning techniques too. These can fit almost any subject and morph around your needs. One of the best is the jigsaw method, discussed below.

Jigsaw Method (usually a whole class period)

This method of engaging students in designing their own learning and teaching others can be highly effective in the college environment. Just do not overuse it or students will feel you aren't doing your own job. Student test scores may increase for the mid and lower range students after a whole class period devoted to using the jigsaw method followed by a test. Again, your brightest students can get frustrated with this method if overused, but students who struggle to find time to study or who have a harder time processing what they read will benefit, sometimes dramatically. This is a tried and true method used extensively in the lower grades. It keeps students actively engaged, gets them to work together with purpose, helps them learn various "study" methods, and be responsible for their own learning. You may want to test right after using the jigsaw, particularly if the class is a long one.

Step One: Prepare study sheets ahead of time with the terms/concepts students need to understand. Don't include answers, just the terms/concepts. Divide these equally between four to six sheets and copy each onto a different color paper. How many sets you make is dependent upon the size of your class and the time you want to allow for the jigsaw.

Step Two: Form initial groups. Pass out your sheets in class, coming as close as possible to having the same number of "A" sheets as "B" sheets, etc. Explain the jigsaw method. Then have all "A" sheet people get together, all "B" sheets form a group, and so on. The job of these initial groups is to look up the information on their study sheet and to make sure that everyone in their group thoroughly understands each term/concept. *They need to fashion a way to remember each concept/term.* They will be teaching the "A" concepts to other students later. Give them time to learn their material. Emphasize they each need to be able to explain it, so they need to practice doing so several times.

Step Three: Form mixed groups. Hopefully you will have only one "A," one "B," one "C," etc. in each group but this varies with class size. You must have at least one member, of course, from each initial study group because each initial group has unique information. Now, students teach their info to each other.

1. Always circulate around and listen in to hunt down and clarify any misconceptions.
2. Always allow students to use their resources so the information they are learning is accurate
3. Emphasize personalization and application as key ways to remember concepts and terms.
4. At the end, you will answer any questions.

Keep it Quality

Whether you use Fast Track activities or long ones, active learning needs to emphasize high quality learning.

To encourage students to give these activities full effort, it's a good idea to consider giving points for something they turn in. The activity points then become your attendance. A simple point allotment (like 1, 2, 3) makes grading fast. Don't give full points to everyone who turns something in. If the work is sketchy, it doesn't deserve them. When quality matters, students will try harder.

Checklist: Active Teaching and Learning

❑ Set students up for success on Day One: discuss expectations, start using groups, review how to read a college text, etc.
❑ Use an applied icebreaker.
❑ Emphasize good study techniques the first day.
❑ Introduce students to the concept of active learning. Explain their role, your role, and why active learning can help them learn faster and remember more.
❑ Plan your lectures out for scheduled interruptions every 10–20 minutes so students practice application of information or answer challenging questions.

❏ Plan your lectures to consciously use the techniques of learning and remembering like stories, visuals, positive emotion, games, etc.

❏ Develop sets of questions for lessons ahead of time. Do not wing it.

❏ Plan a variety of activities: solos, pairs, triads, small groups; all doing many different types of things.

❏ Double check your activities:

❏ Do they relate to the objectives?

❏ Is the challenge level substantial? Requiring critical thinking?

❏ Do they add real value and help students understand? (nothing frivolous or cute)

❏ Can they be finished during class?

❏ Can they be out-processed in the same class?

❏ Is there variety?

❏ Do I have all my props ready? (Like different colored questions and bowls for the Question Bowl Fast Track technique.)

❏ Do I have a set of multipurpose backup activities ready to go?

❏ Have I embedded my great questions into the PowerPoint slides?

❏ Did I develop good apply-sheets for difficult concepts?

❏ Have I designed a couple games for review sessions or downloaded the Jeopardy template?

❏ Have I looked at the entire semester and scheduled out my active learning plans?

❏ Do I have a way to assign points for activities?

Skill 5:

MOTIVATE STUDENTS TO FOCUS ON LEARNING

How do I get students to come to class?
How can I encourage them to do their homework?
How do I get students to participate, be curious, ask questions?

In some version or another, I hear these questions from college teachers over and over again. They all have to do with student motivation. (A topic that frustrates many of us a lot!)

Most people who teach were successful students themselves. They generally liked school and learning, especially when they had classes in their chosen field. Most probably did not have serious attendance problems because they were engaged or at least worried about their grades. Many of our students do not hold these same values, or they are nontraditional students juggling jobs, children, and all the pressures of grownup life. College is squeezed in around the edges.

Understanding some basic motivation principles and being able to apply them in your classes is helpful. You might think students should come to class because they'll learn something; they might need a lot more incentive.

Why should students come to class?

There has to be something in it for them (value) and they have to feel they have a chance to succeed (expectancy). If either component is missing, students will lack motivation.

Basic Expectancy x Value Theory

Students ask:
- Is reaching this goal of any value to me?
- Can I expect to reach the goal if I put forth the effort? Can I expect success in this?
- What's the cost to me in effort, in time, in energy, in self-esteem risk? What else could I be doing with my time and energy that I'll have to give up? (Eccles & Wigfield, 2001)

Students have to perceive a real value to them for attending class.

Students have to feel they can succeed. Costs to them in energy and time must be worth their expenditure.

As an instructor applying this theory,
- Build **value** into each class through a variety of means, especially linking it to students' lives, future careers, etc. with your examples, tips, stories, etc. that genuinely enrich and extend the text.
- Use students' time wisely during each class period.
- Engage them through meaningful active learning techniques they can see are designed to help them master the material and think like professionals in the field.
- Use frequent assessment and feedback to build their likelihood of **success.**
- Set a welcoming and accepting class atmosphere.
- Have realistic expectations for the workload & number of assignments they complete during the semester.
- Make sure homework is directly connected to objectives they need to know; emphasize why and how it builds value to them and will help them succeed in the class.

Beliefs About Ability Impact Effort

My own Ph.D. dissertation dealt with college students' conceptions of ability. I still find this a fascinating area, especially because it is one that impacts student effort and instructors have such influence over it. Here are the basics, put in simple terms. You can read the numerous publications (1983 – current) of C. S. Dweck, E. L. Leggett, and J. Eccles to find out the details.

- Students have a conception about the nature of ability and that conception impacts how much effort they put forth when they hit a "bump" in the road like a test failure.

The two basic conceptions of ability are

Entity
Student idea: I have a "cups" worth of ability. My ability level is "set." Whether it is a large cup (gifted) or a small cup, the cup can't enlarge. Ability isn't malleable. So I have just "so much" math ability. When I hit failure I must have reached the limit of my cup. To put forth more effort is useless and will only hurt my self-esteem. If I don't study at least I can say, "I failed because I didn't study," which saves face.

Incremental
Student idea: Ability is like an unpoppable balloon – the more effort I put in, the bigger the balloon gets, and the more ability I develop. So when I hit failure, that's a clue I need to put forth more effort. I expect effort to build my ability, and failure is not a clue that I'm "at my limit" because ability is malleable.

- Wood and Bandura (1989) did a fascinating study with graduate students and conceptions of ability. On a complex organizational management task, students who had been set up to believe the Entity view rapidly faltered under failure conditions. Students who had been set up to believe the Incremental view did not falter, made better decisions, and showed more positive emotions under the same failure conditions. This is what we want! But what did the researchers do to set up an Entity or Incremental view? They just read a couple sentences, which implied "talent/intelligence" (Entity view) or effort (Incremental view) was the key to success with the task. So simple! But just thinking that their "talent/intelligence" was in question while they were floundering caused the Entity subjects to perform badly.

- Conceptions of ability can vary over subject areas. English, art and math, in particular, are areas where some students feel success happens through some special talent.

KEY: INSTRUCTORS CAN SET UP AN ENTITY OR INCREMENTAL ATMO-SPHERE! Explain conceptions of ability theory to your students. Talk with them about their preconceived notions about what it takes to do well in your subject. Are there people in your class who think success there will depend upon talent? Emphasize that EFFORT, not talent, makes for success.

In the U.S., we have a strong general cultural belief in "talent" and forget to mention the ten years of practice that come before any brilliant performance. So watch your language – it's easy to slip up. Help your students understand people learn at different rates of speed, but with effort almost everyone can attain the knowledge they need in any subject area. Students are fascinated with this theory, and explaining it helps them question their own beliefs and sometimes change poor behaviors. Some students will actually share stories about not studying for tests because they didn't understand and didn't want to feel stupid by studying and then failing. They will verify the theory, particularly with math.

A Nudge in the Right Direction

We are helping students become skilled learners, shaping their behavior over time. After you have set up the best possible active class you can, a slightly behavioral approach to motivation may add that little extra push for good attendance and effort. Most instructors use some system of incentives, rewards, and penalties, even if they don't call them by those names. It really is important to remember that your own system needs to be clearly defined in the syllabus. Students are then choosing the consequences laid out for them.

Attendance issues? First, ask yourself if it is OK with you if students can actually pass your class without attending. If they can, this means you must be teaching straight out of a textbook, adding nothing new, and using only the test bank items. This is rather like a correspondence course. I've met a couple college instructors who felt 100% fine with structuring class this way, and they weren't bothered at all by students only showing up for tests. The point is: don't make attendance mandatory for your own ego – it should be mandatory because students need to be there to get something beyond the textbook information out of the class and to contribute to a learning community of peers. If you aren't going to provide these opportunities for students, then why force them to show up except for tests?

On the other hand, if you are going to set up a participatory, active environment, and you want your students to show up regularly, try these behavioral techniques:

Rewarding Nudges

Continuous reinforcement helps establish a behavior. Give points just for showing up and participating in the in-class activities for the first six sessions or so. Put this information in your syllabus, of course, with the date clearly marked where the "points just for attending" shifts. Students may get into a habit of coming while trying to get all those initial points.

Intermittent reinforcement helps sustain a behavior. This is why people like to continuously pull on those one-armed gambling bandits. They know there will be a reinforcement, they just don't know when. After a period of continuous reinforcement, start intermittent reinforcement by shifting points to activities. Now students do not get points just for showing up anymore.

A GREAT Idea - A philosophy professor I knew had an extremely successful idea for providing intermittent reinforcement for attendance. He had a big, bold spinner wheel with various points from 1 to 10 on it. Each day he made a production of having a student spin the wheel – (it took 30 seconds tops) – and thereby set the points potentially available for the in-class activity of the day. Students cheered and hooted and stomped while the wheel spun, getting their physiology all geared up for a rousing lecture on Plato. Skipping his class could cost you one point, or ten. He had good attendance! [You might be scratching your head about how he computed final grades when activity points weren't the same semester to semester. He used a weighted system. Activities counted for 20% of his class and that remained steady no matter how many points were involved. More on this system in Skill #8, Grading.]

BIG Penalty

A policy that says if students miss more than X classes they earn an automatic F.

SMALLER Penalties

- *Grade those in-class activities* – don't just automatically give everyone all the points for sloppily filling out something. If you don't consider quality it will rapidly diminish for the whole class. If the "wheel spins" and 8 points are available, dole them out somewhat generously, but still according to merit. Some people will not get full points, and they are likely to put more effort out next time.
- *Make in-class activities a significant portion of the semester grade.* Do not allow make-ups on in-class activities unless students have a written doctor or military excuse. The only way to get the points, then, is to come to class. Hold this rule firm. Put this info in the syllabus!
  - ° But DROP the lowest two to four in-class activities. This helps you avoid becoming the one to decide if a mother in the hospital is a "make-up" opportunity but a cousin in the hospital or a dog getting run over is not.
- *Test frequently.* Perhaps give a quiz a week over one chapter. Do not allow make-ups unless students have a doctor or military excuse. All this information needs to be in the syllabus! Again, you may want to drop X number of lowest test scores.
- *Supplement the textbook info.* Give information in class that is an addition to the textbook and then be sure to include it on the tests. Regularly or randomly, this helps. Besides, you are supposed to be an expert – you should be able to add to the text. The key is to test over the new material you add in class.
- *Drop grades for lack of attendance.* For some classes like counseling or interpersonal skills, tests or written in-class products may not be frequent enough to use as an incentive for attendance. If class participation is critical to the whole design of your course, try setting a straight attendance policy that reflects that importance. "Miss three classes – your grade drops one letter grade. Miss five classes – two letter grades." I would not use this in classes that can test, however, because the test then functions in the same manner.

MORE Rewarding Nudges

Honestly, what rewarded you enough to come to class as an undergraduate? You probably were not identical to the average undergrad of today, but think about it anyway and institute some of your own rewards. Was it prompt feedback? Praise in class? The teacher applied the class so well to situations you could relate to that you didn't want to miss anything?

ASK YOUR STUDENTS. Here is a great group activity for Day One or Day Two: *What are the top things that will get you to come to class? Have you ever had a class you just didn't want to miss, ever? Why? What did the teacher do to get you there?* Great questions. You may not find anything startlingly new, but you are including students in a data pool from which you will make policy decisions. Always good practice.

Many people are motivated by positive interaction with the faculty member him/ herself. The teacher knows their names. They talk with them. They know if they aren't there. They deliberately hang around and answer questions and chat after class. They actually seem to care about students as human beings. They come across as a professional, but as a real live breathing human being themselves. They are encouraging. They don't put themselves above the students. They seem to truly value student stories and opinions. The result? When people care about us and are interesting and kind, we don't want to let them down – which spurs getting up at 7:30 to make that 8:00 class for some students.

**Don't underestimate the incentive of basic human interest and kindness.
It's pretty powerful.**

Get Students to Come Prepared for Class

What if students consistently come to class, but they aren't prepared and haven't done their homework? That's pretty frustrating. How do you run group activities that depend on prepared students then?

Some initial suggestions:
- Try to sell the readings for the next class, ahead of time. Tell students how they are going to be important and connect up to what they know and what they will want to know, preview some particularly interesting aspects, etc. Market the material, but don't go over all of it, of course. Build value and interest.
- If students know you are just going to be going over the readings point by point during each class, why should they read to begin with? Never cover everything in the readings in your lecture. Much of the information should be embedded within the activities and discussions you use. Then students must read to participate and understand. (Or at least in theory.)

The FLIPPED Classroom – Dependent on Prepared Students
As a college teacher, you may have already been introduced to the "flipped classroom." In a completely flipped classroom, instructors don't lecture inside the

class, and most class time is spent in application, collaborative and practice activities with the instructor busy helping individuals, groups, etc.

Instructors adopting a flipped system use a variety of methods to get their lecture material across before class: podcasts, recorded lectures, Wikis, videos, PowerPoints with audio, YouTube, etc. They do not tell students just to read the textbook and come to class. They make their "lecture pieces" available to students through the college LMS and students watch or listen to them before class. There are some real advantages here. If you break topics up into different short videos, for example, students can watch a topic they are having trouble with several times. This is a great system (particularly for courses like math and physics) since you would not be repeating yourself over and over and over on the same point in a standard class.

I do have my own doubts about flipping a complete class. It all sounds great but doesn't work so well when half the students show up without having paid a whit of attention to those video lectures you recorded and uploaded. The flipped classroom is dependent on students being well prepared. My decades of experience with students leaves me a little dubious. But we can try, of course.

If you are flipping your class (or even part of your class), you want to do regular readiness assessments to assure students are prepared to go on to the activities in class. This generally means test them! A suggested practice for the flipped classroom is having an individual test completed first and passed in, then small groups do the test again. If someone didn't read, they are at least getting brought up to speed by others who did. The unprepared still suffer point loss on their individual test. You should give immediate feedback on correct answers and explain any troublesome concepts.

Most instructors will not be completely flipping any lecture classroom soon, although incorporating video on-line lectures, PowerPoints with audio, etc. to enhance learning is something all students could benefit from.

Here are incentives to motivate students to come prepared:
1. Start each class with a 10-point quiz over the readings. 10 points, 3-5 minutes, and if you walk in late the test still gets collected with everyone else's. If you come in really late, oops…sorry. (Again, consider dropping X number of these. And cumulatively they have to figure in to at least 10% of the final grade to make studying worthwhile.)

2. Have a couple of interesting essay items posted in the LMS that students have to answer BEFORE coming to class. They should apply directly to the class work and access to them should stop right before class. (Again, must be worth something in points for students to feel the need to do them.) Then discuss these questions in class and feature them in the activities.

3. Place a "worksheet" on the readings/homework into the LMS that students print off and fill out. They need to bring this to class with them. Use the worksheet as material in your activities of the day. Questions combining facts, application, and supported opinion are good. Don't make the workload too big for you or students. Perhaps 10 questions that apply directly to the lesson of the day. Students can use their completed worksheet to help them during activities but can't write more notes on it. Then it gets passed in for points. Or you can have them pass the worksheets in before activities.

4. Variation of the above: let students use their worksheets as a resource on the quiz of the day, but only on random days.

5. Time intensive, but some people do it: Give points for note taking. Collect notes randomly or weekly.

6. Give good points for mind-mapping the readings. Due every class and turned in. (You have to teach them how to mind map first.)

7. Develop your own incomplete outlines or mind maps of the material, all available on the LMS. Students fill out the rest, print off, and bring it to class for points.

8. Give group tests, but group people up who have the worksheets, notes, or mind maps completed to the same level. I've had good success with this one. The students who wrote four pages of notes all got to do the test together. The students who wrote no notes also got to do the test together. (They started coming with real notes eventually!)

9. You can also start the semester giving each student a "preparation point pool." Each time they come unprepared (no essay questions done, no notes, etc., whatever they were supposed to have done isn't done) you deduct points, and after three times coming unprepared, the number of points lost each time goes up.

Over time you will experiment enough to find what works for you and for your students. Realize, however, you will never get ALL your students fully on board exactly the way you'd like them to be. Do your best, keep experimenting, but also be a realist.

Motivate Students to Question and Discuss

If you want better discussion – ask better questions.

We'd all like to encourage students to ask questions if they are puzzled, curious, or confused and would enjoy a rousing discussion involving the whole class. Both goals can be hard to attain. Achieving them requires prep and practice, so expect little success if you "wing it." Yes, that Miracle Day of Wanton Discussion may happen once a semester, but with the right techniques you can have good discussions almost any day.

Get students to <u>ask</u> questions. If you only solicit questions with *"Does anyone have any questions?"* at the end of a long lecture, don't expect good results! Only the boldest will ask anything. Students have been well trained in not asking questions, so you need to shape their behavior into a new pattern. Emphasize that asking questions is how people learn.

- Rather than wait until the lecture's done, break into questioning mode frequently so you don't lose anyone. Model question asking, *"Last year I had a student ask a great question about this: 'If you used XXX rod on this metal what might happen?' Some of you might have the same question, so think about that in pairs; what do you think might happen?"* Attributing the question to a former student and saying it was 'great' shows students you like to get good questions. You can also model curiosity out loud yourself. *"I wonder what would happen if I did XXX? I've never tried that before. What do you think might happen?"*
- In order for students to ask questions, they have to feel free to "not know" publicly. This is hard for some students who are less sure of their abilities, very shy, or care more about what other's think of them. A good solution is to have "huddle time," where little groups get together briefly and come up with questions. No one is on the spot. You can even preface this with: *"You may not have any questions about what we just went over, but think about the general public. What questions might a person ask about this?"*
- How you handle wrong answers or "dumb" questions, then, becomes a signal (positive or negative) to other students. Never put a question down, yet you have to make sure a wise-guy isn't asking off base questions. This is a delicate balancing act. Sometimes asking in a very polite tone, *"How does that question directly apply to XXX which is our subject right now?"* and then waiting in silence will cure such antics.

- Encourage students to speculate a bit about the answer themselves: *"If you were going to speculate, what would you say? What do you think might be the first step, just guessing?"*
- You don't have to answer every question yourself. Throw it open to the students, maybe in pairs: *"Pair up and see if you can speculate on the answer to Joe's question."*
- You might even experiment with giving points for Question Logs over the readings. Instead of normal notes, students write out questions and turn them in.
- Have a question board or question box in the classroom. Students write questions on slips of paper and put them there when they come into or go out of class. You then answer them.
- Probing deeper (asking better follow-up questions yourself) and encouraging students to talk more when they ask a question helps them learn. *"Ok, you have the first part right, but you're a little confused about the XXX – what are some other ideas you have about this? What about XXX made you choose that as the solution?"*

Get students to think harder about their questions: *"What specifically confused you about the concept of XXX in the book?"* If the student says, "the whole thing," you might say, *"ALL of it? Do you understand the X (something easy)?"* Try to get them to think through to a part they actually DO understand rather than just throwing up their hands at the entire thing. Then you have a starting point. You can turn to the class and ask other students to clarify the concept. Some rare students will actually attempt to be annoying or get attention by asking questions over simple materials just to be talking – you want to curtail this activity – and having classmates develop the answer is a good solution.

The types of questions you answer become a signal to the class. In one graduate class, I had a professor answer a fact-based question like this: *"That was in the textbook reading for today. Do you have any other question, something beyond the readings that I can clarify?"* The first time he responded this way the whole class froze, stunned. This was something new. He simply was not going to answer a knowledge-level question on info we could find ourselves if we had read carefully. Believe me, he raised the bar considerably and forced students into thinking deeper about how we phrased our questions! Remember, this was a graduate class. Undergraduates may need a little gentler approach. Still, food for thought. You may find a way to pull this off gracefully and still keep encouraging your students to be curious.

Develop good discussion

Good discussion rarely just happens, but learning to wield this teaching tool effectively is certainly worthwhile to students on many levels.

Benefits of Discussion –
- Students are directly involved
- Students practice expressing themselves
- Students get exposed to various viewpoints
- Students can challenge each other's thinking and stretch themselves considerably
- Students can problem solve as a group and come to deeper understanding

Downsides of Discussion –
- Some students can dominate while others daydream the time away (Find ways to include everyone.)
- Discussions can be unpredictable and shallow, so find questions that demand focus & depth. Keep probing to get beyond shallow thought. Your critical thinking questions centered around intellectual standards and elements of thought (see Skill #6) are perfect for doing this. Teach them to students!
- Discussions can be the "blind leading the blind" – ignorance shared and amplified. (Build knowledge first. Demand sources and tie-backs, not just opinions.)

PLAN AHEAD. Work on your start-up questions, build student knowledge bases, and have an outcome you communicate to students. A good discussion isn't a free-for-all of opinions. Give a little training in asking critical thinking questions to students. In fact (see Skill #6), you should be helping students learn and use critical thinking in every discussion.

If discussion is a major strategy in your class, consider involving students on Day One in a discussion about discussion. In small groups have them brainstorm the worst discussions they have experienced and write down what made them awful. Then have them brainstorm what was going on in the best discussion they've ever experienced. Write that down. Have them come up with some "rules of the road" for good discussions in your class. Collect it, post it, etc. and remind students about it frequently. If discussions go well, point out which of the rules they really stuck to this day. If discussions didn't go well, have them individually look at the rules of the road and write down what they think went wrong, including their own part in it. Collect and use for improvement.

If discussion isn't a major strategy, you still want it to go well when you use it. This still requires preparation time coming up with *questions worth discussing*. It also requires learning a few techniques for drawing the maximum number of people into the talk.

Luckily, no one needs to reinvent the wheel in the area of discussion. There are lots of tips and experts on the web who can help.

- Check out the book by Stephen D. Brookfield, *Discussion as a Way of Teaching: Tools and Techniques for Democratic Classrooms*. Excellent book. If you ever have a chance to go listen to a workshop of Brookfield's – go!
- Don't want to read a book? Check out Stephen Brookfield's website, where he has a large collection of articles and handouts from workshops on discussion techniques. There are more techniques to try than you have time to experiment with in a single semester. They all help maximize the number of people actually talking.

The Great Books system provided the very best discussion class I ever experienced as a student. The professor sold Great Books and organized discussions on them as a young man. He had learned the system well, and we all reaped the benefits. The Great Books discussion groups have a tried and true way of getting the maximum amount of people to lucidly discuss a topic or idea (in this case a book). You can google the process. My professor's interpretation went something like this:

- Ask two provocative questions that students should be prepared for through their readings. Give ten minutes to have students answer them in writing, in class. Let them use their books if you want. Collect.
- Then ask how students responded. The questions you ask them must be open to multiple perspectives and have more than one answer for the discussion to be good.

Practical Tips for Great Discussion

- Give individual time first. One commonality among many good techniques is letting people have individual time to think about a question first and jot a few notes to themselves – and then let them talk with a small group before breaking into a larger group for sharing and a general discussion. This allows people to get their thoughts in order and helps out shyer students who may rarely participate in the free-for-all of the common classroom discussion.
- Keep dominators at bay. Another excellent idea is to have some sort of system in place that keeps two people from dominating the entire discussion time. One suggestion is a "talking stick," which gets passed around. If you

hold the stick, you get to talk. If you aren't holding the stick, you listen intently. You can even put a limit on times to hold the stick. If talkative students only have three times they can actually talk, they will learn to hold back and let others take a turn, and the comments they make may become more focused and relevant.

- Get students to pay attention to others. Try a "round robin" discussion. For whole classes, one student starts, then the student sitting next to them reiterates the point they made (or disagrees with it, etc.) and adds their own information, on around the class. People start to pay attention to what others are saying, at least those talking right before them! You can also do this in small groups (less threatening), with a report back to the class.
- Small groups before large groups. Try challenge questions for groups. Design three questions, divide class into three groups, each with one question, set a timer, and have a representative from each group report back at the buzzer. Students talk more to each other. Three different questions helps keeps the large group discussion fresh too, with less repeating.
- Use only the upper levels of Bloom for discussion questions. Fact items don't work. Teach students to probe for clarity, depth, hidden assumptions…to use critical thinking questions to expand discussions and keep them going in new or deeper directions. Try to avoid *"What did you think of this book?"* in favor of *"Do you agree or disagree with this quote from page 34? Why? What are the assumptions behind the quote? What do you think the author's purpose was here?"*
- Choose good starter questions. What makes a question worthy of discussing? Complexity and no simple answer. The very best questions are those the instructor him/herself is still pondering. Those are real questions, not "pretend" questions where the right answer is already known.
- Emphasize informed opinions. Students need to understand the difference between pure opinion and backing up their impressions or conclusions with data from the material: *"What information from the readings helped you form that opinion?"* or *"…gave you this impression?"*
- Keep discussion going once it gets started. Brookfield has an excellent handout on questions to keep discussion going. I took it to class with me! Questions as simple as *"Can you give us another example?"* keep discussion going. But you can also figure out a lot of good questions by looking through critical thinking materials. Questions like *"Take someone else's point of view on this, someone we are leaving out so far, what would they think?"* Or a question chain for a whole class: *"If we took your solution all the way out and the world actually implemented this, what would change? What else? What would be some other positive changes? Negative changes? Who would oppose this*

solution? Why would they? How do you know that?" (Skills #4 and #6 list more good questions to adapt for your classes.)

- Stay ahead. Come with more questions than you need.
- Help students learn to ask better questions of their classmates: *"What can we ask Brad to get a better handle on what he is saying?" "...to better understand how he drew this conclusion?"* You can give them a list of general questions to ask while they are learning.
- Keep class civil. Don't allow a safe class atmosphere to be harmed by anyone or discussion may halt for the rest of the semester. You may need civility ground rules. Some students think they are being funny with sarcasm and critiques (verbal or nonverbal), but these are discussion bombs in the long run.

Seating Arrangements Impact Interaction

Maximum interaction doesn't happen when students are looking at the backs of heads. If there is any way you can alter the seating in your classroom to facilitate active discussion with peers, eyeball to eyeball, do so. You might be staggered at how much the classroom dynamics change with a change in seating.

If you do not have a dedicated classroom for your sole use, you'll have to get to class early to move chairs, but the results are worth your effort. Students will help, too, because they appreciate the class atmosphere created.

- A large circle works if you don't have a huge class. Two circles inside one another are better than classic seating with everyone looking at the board. For seminar or discussion-based classes, try a single circle if the room allows it.
- A large "U" works. Two "U"s inside each other work (great for large classes). Anything to get people looking mostly into the eyes of other students. For classes that still need to be looking up at you or the board for part of the class, go with the "U"s.
- Double circles offer some interesting activity possibilities. For a first question, have only the inner circle answer and discuss. Have the outer circle take notes. You might even give them a specific set of questions to answer about the discussion. For the second part, have the outer circle rebut points made by the inner circle or extend their points, etc. You can come up with many ways to utilize two circles. One tip: stagger the seats so the outer circle participants can still be seen by almost everyone because they are sort of "between but behind" two members of the inner circle. Be sure to switch up who is in each circle.

- Don't settle for an arrangement that lets some students hide or turn their backs to you. Tables with chairs set around them force some students to sit with their backs to you or to sit at right angles to their note-taking materials. This isn't a good situation to inspire attention and engagement. Rearrange.
- Arrange seating with an eye to small group in-class activities. You want a speedy movement from lecture to active learning activity. The double "U" setup, for instance, allows the inner "U" to turn rapidly around and form groups with the outer "U." No getting up and milling about the class, wasting time. To get new groups, the inner people can just stand up and move over six seats…presto…mostly new faces. Works super well.
- Notes and laptops. I walked by a classroom one time and saw screen after screen of solitaire, email, and Facebook. The professor was at the front of the room working through a problem on the board. I was looking in through a window at the back. It was hardly a learning situation for all students. If you do decide to care about this issue, you want to set your classroom up so you can see monitors. Also, I feel you can ask students who say they need a laptop to take notes to justify that by emailing their notes to you after every class period. Otherwise, no laptops. If they are actually taking notes that won't be a problem for them.

Disruptive Students

Besides the seating arrangement, there are other considerations when you are responsible for classroom dynamics. Think about all the annoying students you met over your years as an undergraduate and expect to meet their doubles in your classes – plus many variations. Plan ahead and include policies in your syllabus for situations that disturb the learning environment. When disruptive students get away with their behaviors, other students can become unhappy and unmotivated. They will blame you for not being able to handle someone who is messing with the class.

Sleepers

Yes, sometimes people sleep in class. Should you let them? What kind of toll does snoring take on other students' ability to concentrate? Sleeping can impact class dynamics. But this is an easy one to get around if you address it on the first day, humorously.

In my opening spiel, I always mention that I don't tolerate sleepers. I say, *"I'll come kick you if you fall asleep in my class."* This always gets a laugh, and I tell them I'm quite serious, but I'll only nudge their foot – the first time. If it continues, I'll ask them to stand up, or leave if they need to. They obviously need more sleep and can't get anything out of class or contribute to anyone else's learning. I present this sympathetically, not rudely. Then I follow through. Even though I have active classes, I've had occasional sleepers during lecture. I walk over quietly, nudge their foot gently while the class looks on wide-eyed, and wake them up.

You have to have great rapport for this to work and not offend anyone, so I do suggest caution. You might not quite be able to pull this off yet (I do have grand-motherly grey hair), but you can wake students in another acceptable manner. Move close to where they sit and start talking more loudly. "Accidentally" drop something noisy up front. Switch to a small group by using a bell. Usually the student will wake up. The idea is to wake them, not tick them off or humiliate them.

Talk privately with someone who seems to frequently fall asleep. They may have a medical condition or perhaps worked the night shift and are staying awake for your 10 a.m. class before falling into bed. Ask them what might help – a different spot in the room? Ice to crunch? Permission to stand in the back? You can try to help them rather than blame them.

Rude Talkers

Early on, discuss the issue of students chatting while you are talking or while other students are sharing. Let students discuss how annoying this is to them and solutions they've seen in other classes – the good and the ugly. Come to a class consensus on how to handle this problem and then *stick to it*. Assure students they'll have plenty of time together during group activities so they can hold their casual thoughts for a little while. This helps!

You will always have the opportunity to hone your skills handling the chatting problem because each semester it happens again. Some instructors stop talking and just stare at the culprits until they finally shut up. Others go over and ask them to share whatever it is that is so interesting. You'll find your own pattern. Just don't tolerate such disruption because it really annoys other students who are actually trying to listen. It's rude. Put a policy in your syllabus.

Defuse Troublemakers Early – They Ruin Participation

Even in college, you'll have them occasionally – troublemakers. Some are just immature, some may have mental/emotional challenges, and others seem out to make your life miserable. They don't come along very frequently (thank good-ness), but they must be dealt with swiftly and fairly or they harm the learning environment for everyone. If you identify a potential troublemaker early, sometimes you can go out of your way to give them extra attention after or before class in an attempt to build personal rapport. Get them on your side. Mention a point they made that was really good. Many times this will avert a problem and you'll turn them into a fan.

Going head-to-head in class with a true troublemaker or troubled student is not a good solution. Many of these students do not have the same social restraints you do, allowing them to "win." Some have little impulse control. Negative encounters between students and instructors are terribly disturbing to the whole class. If you have trouble with a student wait for him/her after class, take the student to one side and ask if they can meet a minute in your office. ALWAYS keep your office door open!

Discuss your feelings about their behavior. Use classic "I messages." *I feel disrespected when you do such-and-such....* Emphasize how their behavior is disrupting the class and how students have complained or appear uncomfortable. Identify the *specific behaviors* that are disruptive. Don't just say, *"you're being immature"*. Don't label the person. In general, most obnoxious students do not know how they are perceived. Many just think they are being terribly clever. Finding out other students are annoyed rather than entertained and that their instructor is unhappy with them is sometimes a surprise.

Be prepared ahead of time so you can finally refer to policies in the student handbook regarding behavior and consequences. Stay courteous and respectful even if they are not. Keep your cool in all ways. Tell them what they need to do to remain in the class. Ask them what you need to do to help them adjust to class better. This will usually (not always) cure the situation. Keep notes of what transpired. Type them up right after the student leaves so you remember everything. If you feel the situation isn't going to resolve itself, share the notes with your supervisor.

If you are ever uncomfortable approaching a student alone, ask your Dean of Instruction, Dean of Students, or a Counselor to be with you. Hold the meeting in their office, not yours. If you can't get a student to meet with you at all, go to the Dean of Students. They will help. If a student seems dangerous in any way, tell your supervisor plus the Dean of Students, and hold this meeting in the security administrator's office.

Skill 6:

HELP STUDENTS LEARN TO LEARN AND THINK CRITICALLY

One of the greatest gifts you can offer students is to help them learn how to learn. Many students come to college with no real knowledge of basic techniques that will help them learn. Even some top students flounder in college because high school was so easy for them they don't really know how to be self-directed learners. If you want students to learn to learn, the opportunities to do so have to be an integrated part of your class.

One major way to accomplish this goal is to have students generate meaningful questions about the material they are studying and then research deeply until they can answer them. The more connected to real life problems the questions are, the more students will want to spend the energy to discover the answers. The answers become important to them. An extreme example: imagine a nursing student, slogging along, not really working too hard – and suddenly her child is diagnosed with Type I diabetes. Her entire attitude will likely change about research and studying. She will look for every possible study on Type I diabetes, learning what makes a good study, how media reports differ from study outcomes, what new treatments are available, etc. She wants real, verified information, not snake-oil hype, and in doing this research, she will learn to tell the difference. This topic has become wildly relevant to her life and she will become an expert on it. She is emotionally invested. In the process she has learned how to learn.

Certainly, our classes won't generate the passion of a mother or father trying to help their child! I get that. But I gave an extreme example to drive home a point: students learn to be self-teachers when they are invested. This requires that we give them some choice in assignments, don't spoon feed information, and continually push them to ask meaningful questions they actually want to answer.

We need to realize many of our inexperienced students also need the absolute basics of how to study. There is still classroom learning to master. A textbook to read. Tests to study for. We aren't going to turn students into self-teachers the first week of the semester, but we can help them develop the study skills to retain in college long enough to get there.

It is a good idea to review study techniques in your class during the first weeks. The ideas below are from educational psychology research and are sound approaches to helping students learn how to learn. These seem so elemental, but I recommend going over each of these topics. You can make a game of it, or a lively discussion, but however you choose to approach these, you are doing yourself and your students a service.

Daily Commitment

- Seems obvious, but inexperienced students frequently procrastinate and don't realize 30 minutes a day adds up. I joke with students and tell them to haul their psychology book everywhere so they can read at red lights, in waiting rooms, and in the bathroom. They groan, but when we add up the minutes it is substantial over a week.
- Emphasize how important it is to study when alert, not exhausted. Studying when exhausted is usually ineffective. When doing "zombie reading" you can't process the information. Reading at 2 a.m. is usually worthless unless you are truly a night hound. How about getting up a little earlier and reading 15 minutes with a cup of coffee? This would be a major step forward if your brain functions alertly in the morning. What students need to do is find their own "alertness sweet spot" and study in it.
- Share the Premack Principle = "Eat your peas before you can have dessert." A less desired behavior is linked to a more rewarding behavior. Talk to students about self-discipline, attaining goals, and using the Premack principle to teach themselves this vital trait. An hour of study before play is something a few will actually try. After such a display of self-control, one can play without nagging guilt and really enjoy it. Massively successful people have developed a system of self-discipline that works for them. Massively successful students do the same thing.

Reading and Studying

I've had many students over the years bomb a test and then come up and say, "But I read the whole chapter!" Reading is not studying. We can put this in perspective for students: if reading were studying you could pass a test on any newspaper, book, or magazine article you'd read casually sitting in a waiting room. We get introduced to the information in a chapter by reading it, but thinking about it, answering questions, writing down bits, drilling on terms, deliberately making linkages to things already known or personal, reviewing, rereading, asking ourselves questions – these are the techniques of studying.

- Tell students to PREVIEW: to flip through the chapter first, reading the headings, under the photos, examining the charts, and reading any summary information. This PREVIEW orients the student to the material and helps them make connections when they do a more thorough reading.
- Have students ask and answer questions as they read. A good textbook might ask questions along each page edge; you might provide some questions; or a student study guide might be available for your textbook. This gets more interaction going with the material.
- Encourage students to reflect as they read, to try to apply what they are reading to something they already know. This is a vital skill for remembering information. The more connections, the easier memory storage and retrieval happen. (You, of course, can provide them with homework in the form of questions that focus on application, connections, etc.)
- Explain the serial position effect. We remember the beginning and end of information more readily than information in the middle. Thus, breaking chapters up into small segments to read (rather than reading a whole chapter all at once) means we will remember more. You want to create more beginnings and more ends.
- Encourage distributed practice (little bits over time) because it works better than cramming (lots at once). If you think about long-term memory as a swimming pool, cramming puts information into the shallow end where it can leap out quickly. Distributed practice puts information closer to the deep end where it has a chance to remain.
- Students should highlight and underline as they read– but not too much. Less highlighting actually correlates to higher learning. Students are forced to identify the main issues rather than blindly color a whole paragraph yellow, and when they review, there the main points are.

Remember, your job isn't to give out information, it is to facilitate student learning. So whatever you can do to help students learn will eventually make you more successful too. If you can help shape reluctant students' studying behaviors by offering points for answering questions from the text, reflections, mind maps, outlines, etc., so much the better. Frequently what gets Points gets Done.

Remembering and Memorizing

You want students to remember all that important information, not just barely memorize it shallowly for a test and forget it. Students have to be active about putting information into their long term memory to *remember,* and from there it can be recalled. Making information personal, visual, connected, important, and practiced will help anyone remember. Many of your active learning activities and assignments will do just this.

Some things in college will have to be memorized through direct effort especially in the foundational classes. A Nobel Prize winning chemist probably had to memorize the Periodic Table at some point.

- Help students learn the principle of overlearning – which is simply to go over and over and over way past the point you know something to make it "yours." Pianists do this. Singers do this. Stage actors do this. Quarterbacks do this. They overlearn by practicing over and over and over. They think they know it? They rehearse twenty more times. Or two hundred more times.
- Flash cards are our friends. (Wonderful tools for overlearning.) Flash cards have been made fun of, but that's because too much schooling focused exclusively on facts. We need some facts in order to build the higher levels of cognition, and flash cards are good tools for drilling them in. However, flash cards are good for more than facts. They can hold multiple explanations, critical questions on the material, pros and cons, metaphors, etc. You can make games like "Name That Disease" out of flash cards. Symptoms on one side, diagnosis on the other. Flash cards? Yes!
- The web has fabulous resources on memory techniques, for free.
- In fact, some of your students are already highly skilled at memorizing information. Find a panel of expert memorizers within your own class and have them explain how they do what they do. Some people do not know they are expert memorizers because they think only of academic information. But how many people know all the information out there about a specific baseball team? Or all the lyrics to hundreds of songs? This requires memory. So they actually have the skill – let them know they can transfer it into the academic arena if they identify how they did it to begin with (frequently a lot of repetition and a lot of personal interest).
- Many of your best memorizers use mnemonic techniques. Remember what Roy G. Biv stands for? If you ask this question in class, most of your students know the answer: the color spectrum, in order. That's a mnemonic they

learned in elementary school, and it is still with them in college because it was repeated so many times. Have groups come up with mnemonic devices for some challenging material during the semester – you get people to learn a great memorization technique and the content at the same time.

• When you test, always include important material from previous tests. Students need to continually recall information about a subject to process it into long term memory. Test cumulatively so students must study material more than once.

Note Taking

Clever, current research supports note taking as a positive way to not only help students learn and remember, but to help them score better on tests. But students seem reluctant. They want your PowerPoints. They will demand or plead for your class notes, study guides, test review sheets, etc. to avoid taking their own notes. Yes, some students will even stare at you when you say, "You might want to take notes on this part," but they don't lift a finger. Is this because they haven't a clue how to take notes, or in their frame of reference, is it just too uncool/been unnecessary/didn't help them? But note taking *will* help them, so we need to teach it.

Mind mapping for Notes

The concept of mind mapping as a note-taking tool is new to most students. Many were taught to take notes with the standard old I, II, III, IV, a. b. c. outline method. Remember when the teacher told you if there wasn't enough information for a "b" that you couldn't have just an "a"? Many students try to take notes with this old method. The problem with outlining with the old method is that it doesn't fit the way our minds actually work. We aren't totally lineal thinkers and many times we do have "a" in our thoughts without "b." Instead of lineally, we think in patterns. We think in images. Our brains love images, pictures, visuals. We can remember a good picture far easier than an outline of words.

Mind mapping takes what we know about memory and the brain and turns it into a satisfying note taking system that truly makes sense. When students use color and draw little doodles of their thoughts within the mind map, it works even better. The only problem with mind mapping? People are reluctant to learn something new, even when it will actually help them learn faster and remember more. This technique takes effort and thinking to master. Yes, research in mind mapping does find those results. Now if we can just get people to do it!

Model mind mapping yourself as you cover material. That way you are demonstrating the technique. Draw the mind-map as you talk rather than have it all done. If you are using a document camera or similar tool, you can have a completed mind map sitting on the podium to glance at while you draw the one students can see as you go through your lecture. This is actually more effective than seeing the entire mind map at the start. Students pay more attention as they get to watch the building process unfold.

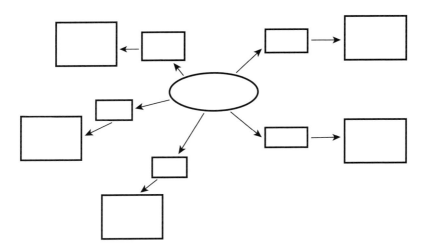

Offer points for mind maps or, as suggested earlier in this book, let small groups take some tests together, grouped up by the completeness of their mind maps.

"Teacher" Notes

Another way to take notes on a chapter is to start thinking like a teacher: *"This is an important point. How can I make a test question out of it? How can I teach it?"* Show students how to use a spiral notebook (or a beloved software) for this project. Make three columns on a page. Column 1 is for Information. Column 2 is for a Test Question. Column 3 is for PIECE: Personal – Image – Experience – Connection – Example (all ways to help us remember). As students read, they take their notes inside the columns. They try for at least one of the PIECE techniques, not all of them. The notes students take this way are quite individual and may not be completely understood by someone else. When students want to study for a test, they cover up Column 1 and start asking themselves their own test questions.

Information	Test Questions	PIECE
• 3 types of mammals	• what are the 3 types of mammals?	• Emi had pups, placenta, nursed them
• placental	• which has the fewest members?	• we = placentals, nursing in restaurants
• monotreme		• mono (round o = egg laying)(fewest)
• marsupial	• examples of each?	• marsupial=kangaroos=pouches

Reflection, Summary, and Note Taking

If you give points for note taking in some form or another, add in a requirement for summaries and reflection. The research on note taking certainly supports it is the process of grappling with the material (not the act of taking notes) that makes the difference:

"….it is the process, the engagement with the material – the cognitive exercise involved in recollecting, summarizing, reorganizing and restructuring [the notes] that actually matters the most." (Cohen, D.; Kim, E.; Tan, J.; and Winkelmes, M. (2013). p. 98)

Bodies, Emotions, and Remembering

- Extremely stressful situations foster high anxiety and inhibit learning. You need to find the right balance between "good stress" and challenge. Put students into situations that stretch them, but don't put them under high threat. This might be the difference between solving a difficult math problem as a group instead of as an individual whose self-esteem is then at risk in front of others.

- When we are emotionally involved, our chances of learning more are heightened. Why? We're probably more alert to begin with, and attention itself is the critical first step to learning. No attention = no potential for learning. Emotions also trigger a whole sequence of chemicals in the body and brain that have powerful effects on learning/remembering. Fear triggers fight or flight responses, which are not exactly conducive to higher-order thinking. Emotions are part of us; you can't separate them from learning in general. So how can you use this knowledge to aid learning? Applications to real life and case studies can help with building positive emotion, as can humor. Students need to feel they can make mistakes, take risks with questions, etc. in your classroom. Students do not have to have 'fun' all the time to learn, but they do need to feel emotionally involved and emotionally safe.

- Unpleasant emotional experiences with a subject can impede our ability to approach it openly now and into the future. The math-class-from-hell in high school thus is connected to feelings about math in college, "anchoring" a new math class to the bad feelings from a past math class. How can you help students overcome this?

- Our bodies are part of the learning process. When students are dehydrated, poorly fed, exhausted, or otherwise challenged physiologically, learning is harder. Talk to them about this. Particularly talk with them about the need for full hydration and sleep. There is good research in this area you can tap in to and share. In addition, involve the body in learning activities. Movement and physical engagement are positive ways to enhance learning. This can be as simple as having groups hang their answers to a challenge in different places around the room and then having the groups walk around together and evaluate them. Thinking + movement. Good combo.

- We like meaning. Our brain craves meaning. Our brain seeks patterns and connections. Unrelated bits of information are hard to memorize and harder to recall. So the more we make connections between old and new information the better our chances of helping students deeply understand, process, and recall the new information. Don't assume students can link up old and new information themselves just because you can – many can't. You'll have to help them out.

- We learn with our whole brain – not just the "left side" or "right side," although certain processes are more "focused" in one hemisphere or the other. We need to engage "both sides," the "whole brain" in as many ways as possible. Using a wide variety of active teaching and learning techniques can do this. Stories and images (graphs, charts, photos) to support information also help whole brain learning.

- Personally meaningful information is processed differently and will be retained. We have different types of memory and can memorize an amazing array of information, retaining it for brief or long periods of time, depending upon how it is processed. We can memorize a lot with our "rote" memory areas, but this info generally is not retained for long or may be difficult to recall fairly rapidly. If we want *learning,* not just memorization, then we need to make information meaningful and put it in context for students. We also need to help students take control of "personalizing" information – we can do this through careful application questions and activities such as building metaphors.

Critical Thinking – The Greatest Gift

Help students become critical thinkers and they will make better decisions throughout their lives. They will become much more astute consumers of information from any source. They will be able to evaluate claims, arguments, reasoning, etc., cutting through the bias, manipulation, and logical fallacies that are so much a part of daily communication. When citizens think critically, an entire culture benefits.

However, the classic lament around the faculty copy machine is *"These students can't think!"* Well, maybe most of your students really can't think critically yet, but they can learn to. It is part of your job to teach students to think critically within your field. There is an entire collection of little books that can help you in this endeavor, published by The Foundation for Critical Thinking (see Resource list in back). They are so good, in fact, I recommend you consider using at least one as a supplemental text in your classes. Each costs only a few dollars. Every student can afford them. But these little books cover a sweep of information without any fluff and will enhance your assessment, your discussion techniques, your questioning skills, and students' abilities to approach their lives thoughtfully.

The Miniature Guide to Critical Thinking, Concepts and Tools is the shortest book in Dr. Richard Paul and Dr. Linda Elder's series. There are also specific titles on *Scientific Thinking, Engineering Thinking, Asking Essential Questions, Analytic Thinking, Clinical Reasoning,* and others. All excellent and usable. The information in each overlaps, so you do not need the whole set. Their intellectual standards for assessing the *quality* of thinking are presented in each book: Clarity, Precision, Accuracy, Relevance, Depth, Breadth, Logic, Fairness, and Significance. These quality standards are applied to the elemental structure of reasoning: Purpose (all reasoning has a purpose), Point of View (do I know mine or consider others?), Assumptions (which assumptions are influencing my reasoning?), Question (the key question to answer), Information (needed to answer the question), Concepts (the basic concepts to clarify and understand for this question), Inferences (basic conclusions), Implications (of this line of reasoning).

> "Intellectual standards are essential to the assessment of thinking. Most students cannot name a single standard they use to assess thinking. It is therefore important to bring intellectual standards into daily classroom activities. One way to move in this direction is to routinely ask students questions that require them to apply intellectual standards to their thinking:

I'm not clear about your position. Could you state it in other words? (clarity)

Can you articulate how you have considered the complexities in the issue? (depth)

Have you focused on the most significant issue in dealing with this problem? (significance)."

P. 40 *A Miniature Guide on How to Improve Student Learning*

Key Points

- Students really do need to understand what an unbiased source is and what the difference is between opinion and evidence. In our current mainstream American culture this is actually quite challenging to get across as TV personalities have an opinion about everything, many times taken as fact. But unless students can understand the difference between biased and unbiased sources, and casual opinion versus expert evidence, they will not be critical thinkers.

- Model critical thinking for your students *obviously* and continually demonstrate how thinking is done in your field of study. That means you need to learn to talk out loud about your own thinking. You can't expect the unskilled thinkers sitting in front of you to pick out assumptions and inferences in your thought processes especially if your conclusions are in any way opposed to their own preconceived notions. (They will have roadblocks up.)

- What do you say when you talk out loud? I'd suggest you don't wing it, but think through this yourself beforehand so you are sure to include the intellectual standards and elements of reasoning quite explicitly: *"Well, when faced with this design problem, first I have to ask myself – really, what is my purpose here? What question shows the key problem?"*

- Develop lecture interrupters for pairs or groups out of the elements of thought: What is the *purpose* of X? What *question* is really at issue here? What *information* do we have, or need to get? Certainly the author came to a conclusion here, was it *justified by the evidence* presented? Could there be an *alternative conclusion* given the same evidence? These are challenging questions and will engage groups and individuals. If you have any one of the Critical Thinking series in your hands, these types of questions will come easily to you.

- When you develop rubrics for papers, etc. remember to always include critical thinking as one of the criteria you expect. But be sure to break down critical thinking into manageable bits so students get meaningful feedback about those areas of critical thinking they are building skills up in and those still needing work. "Critical thinking" is composed of a set of many different skills. Students will master some before others.

- Develop larger activities that help students understand and recognize the elements of thought and intellectual standards in current events. You could have a lot of fun with this one by making little audios or videos while "haranguing" on a topic "without thought" and then have students dissect them. (Perhaps you have an Uncle you could record talking about the fur trade, the Farm Bill, or politics!) OR, just look in your local newspaper's Letters to the Editor column. I had a great deal of fun using a series of letters to the editor on the subject of urban chickens in my critical thinking classes. I believe over the course of two weeks we covered almost every possible turn in unskilled thinking examples. Students had fun and learned valuable lessons by ferreting them out.

Get students to
- Think about the complexity of issues, emphasizing the influence of multiple variables *[What are all the variables that may influence how a person reacts to a piece of art? …impacts safety in the construction phase? …influences a credit rating?]*
- Think abstractly
- Think about long term consequences, build cause and effect chains, speculate/predict
- Self-reflect about their own thinking
- Challenge their own beliefs and assumptions
- Practice playing devil's advocate (students take an opposite side for debates, position papers, discussions – but collecting valid information first)
- Shift from reasoning based on personal beliefs to the use of unbiased evidence
- Identify assumptions in others' reasoning
- Collaborate with others, work in groups, hear numerous points of view
- Participate more in class and at a higher cognitive level

Checklist: Developing Motivated, Thinking Students

- ❑ Plan a means to ask students their interests and goals so you can bring up examples during the semester that touch upon them, building value.
- ❑ Structure your classes to maximize student participation.
- ❑ Develop a seating arrangement that facilitates discussion and attention.
- ❑ Develop a method to learn student names rapidly.
- ❑ Give a presentation on Entity and Incremental Conceptions of Ability.
- ❑ Plan for frequent assessment and frequent feedback. Schedule quizzes and tests in small bites.

❑ Develop "new" material (not covered in the textbook) to add to each class. Test over it.

❑ Make in-class activities a significant portion of grade.

❑ Develop a simple rubric or other system for grading in-class activities.

❑ Plan your grading system with an eye to motivation: nudging students in the best direction.

❑ Put your incentives, penalties and rewards into the syllabus.

❑ Consider arranging to videotape a couple of your classes for your own enlightenment.

❑ Be motivating yourself: love your job, your subject, and enjoy your students. Enthusiasm is contagious.

❑ Try to use more incentives than punishments.

❑ Consider dropping some of the lowest scores for frequent tests and activities.

❑ Use a variety of techniques to get students to ask questions.

❑ Plan ahead for good discussion. Have your technique and questions ready to go.

❑ Handle disruptive students professionally but rapidly so they don't harm the learning environment.

❑ Review how to study and how to remember with students.

❑ Work with students so they learn how to take notes. Consider making notes worth points.

❑ Adopt a critical thinking booklet from The Foundation for Critical Thinking [see Resources] and use it.

❑ Practice modeling good critical thinking out loud. Students need to hear you thinking so they will learn to.

❑ Craft critical thinking questions into every lecture, every activity, and every discussion.

❑ Include self-reflection, cause and effect, identifying assumptions, etc. as activities.

❑ Insert critical thinking into all your grading rubrics.

❑ Integrate self-teaching across your curriculum and include it on rubrics.

Skill 7:

DEVELOP MULTIPLE WAYS
OF ASSESSING LEARNING

What? A Midterm and Final Isn't Enough?

There are huge books written on assessment. I would bet your college library has one of the best: *Classroom Assessment Techniques* by Thomas Angelo and Patricia Cross. When you have time, check it out. It is an excellent resource as you develop your skills. In *Win Them Over Faster* I am attempting to give you an overview of assessment, not create the definitive work on it. Therefore I am focused on clear useful advice you can put into practice immediately.

Purpose

The true purpose of assessment is *meaningful change that positively impacts student learning* – not giving students a grade. Good assessment, timed well, drives changes in our instructional strategies and curriculum development to benefit student learning.

WHAT we assess influences how students study. If we only test over little facts and figures, students will study with the intent in mind to memorize the little facts and figures. Because of this intent they frequently won't see any of the bigger picture or understand connections or really grasp why the very information they are studying is important. But if you ask complex test questions that require a deeper understanding, then students will have the intent of looking for those things when they study. Ask questions that associate facts and concepts as well as translate the theoretical into 'real life' and students will start studying to pass those tests. Intent is quite a powerful guide to how we read and study. Know what you want to accomplish when you design tests. Do you want students to be able to connect something from Chapter 4 with the new information from Chapter 6? Ask the right questions to achieve that aim. What you assess gets done.

Four Key Terms in Practice

Formative Assessment – Your "Early-Warning" Guidance System

Missiles used to have a guidance system telling them when they were "off target" all along their trajectory and adjustments were made so they landed on the right spot. Formative assessment does exactly the same thing for you. It tells you if students are on track with learning and helps you know where to adjust so they land on the right spot. Another comparison: Formative assessment is the thermometer a nurse sticks in a patient's mouth. It is a tool that gives information on how the patient is doing during a hospitalization. Is the temperature up too high? The doctor revises treatment based on the information from the thermometer. Formative assessment goes on throughout the semester (just as nurses take temperatures daily). These assessment efforts tell you what/how much your students understand so you can make adjustments to teaching and activities to help them when they flounder. Formative assessment is diagnostic, showing you where something needs improvement. Formative assessment is usually not graded (or has minimal points) and frequently is turned in anonymously. With formative assessment, the *meaningful change that positively impacts student learning* happens <u>now</u> while the current crop of students is still sitting in your class.

Summative 'Assessment' – The Evaluation of Student Outcomes

This is the type of assessment all instructors are familiar with: evaluation = grades. The final summing up generally comes at the end of the semester, but pieces of summative assessment are usually liberally sprinkled throughout the course and may include components like participation and attendance. Evaluation is "high stakes," and students want it fair, clear, and highly connected to the objectives of the class. When you are performing summative evaluation, you judge student work for quality and generate the final grade. With summative evaluation, the *meaningful change that positively impacts student learning* happens <u>later</u> when you examine how the current crop of students did and plan adjustments to benefit next semester's students.

Please don't get hung up on the terms *assessment* and *evaluation*, which people at colleges frequently use interchangeably. Focus on the terms Formative (*I have the chance to re-Form my instructional strategies so students learn more before the final exam!*) and Summative, as in *I have to <u>sum up</u> their scores and give The Grade.* Formative assessment happens all semester; summative evaluation arrives at a final grade.

Direct Measures – *Show Me Exactly What You Learned*

Direct measures actually "directly" measure student learning on the course outcomes. Such direct measures involve a wide swath of possibilities for both formative and summative assessment. A direct measure could be a demonstration of a skill – a final paper graded on a rubric – a project which demonstrates one essential objective – a verbal presentation explaining the relationship between two concepts – or 80 hours of clinical where students directly show they can do the work of nurses with live patients. It doesn't get more direct than that. In all these cases, a student must demonstrate their skill/knowledge/understanding.

Indirect Measures – *Tell Me…Something*

Indirect measures do not result in the same kind of "show me what you know" assessments. Indirect measures can only *infer* what skill/knowledge/understanding students actually have. Surveys asking students how much they learned – surveys asking employers if graduates know such-and-such – graduation rates – employment rates – student satisfaction inventories – student evaluations of your class – student comments about how much an activity helped them – all these are indirect measures. They are not direct proof of student learning, but they do give information which might help instructors re-vision teaching techniques, curriculum, and program offerings in the future.

At the course level, your assessment should be focused primarily on direct measures, not indirect measures. Although we all like to know if students enjoy our courses, enjoyment is not the essential outcome we are looking for because it does not equate to knowledge, understanding, or skills. We need to know if students mastered the learning objectives for our course by having them show us they did.

Direct Formative Assessment Techniques (CATS or Classroom Assessment Techniques)

Double Dip with Active Instructional Strategies

Under Skills #3 and #4, numerous active instructional strategies were shown that easily double as Direct Formative Assessments. Activities like Pro/Con, Similarities/Differences, Similes, and Comparisons of two theories/concepts/objects/protocols etc. can be both challenging activities for small groups or pairs, and can be used for formative assessment of individuals. What makes an activity a formative assessment? *How you use it.* An instructional activity is used to break up lecture and get students applying and thinking about the material immediately. If you look at the data that comes back with an eye to re-forming something about your lesson if needed, then you are also using that activity in a formative manner. Double dipping is terrific use of time!

Use formative techniques all semester long but only when you are teaching a challenging concept. There is no point doing a CAT over something you know the class understood easily. You need several different techniques or you will bore your students. Variety adds spice and helps you look at student learning from many different angles. If you craft direct formative assessments well, they also serve as great challenging activities to keep students engaged and thinking.

Should you give points for CATS? Your choice. Many instructors do not. Others feel their students will not take CATS seriously without a point or two attached. Certainly the points should be very minimal. You aren't trying to "Grade;" you are trying to see if students understand in time to fix it if they don't. Very different outcomes from graded assignments.

Should CATS be anonymous all the time? Again, your choice. It depends upon what you will do with the data. If you are teaching math and want to know who is missing something so you can work with them individually, then names are appropriate. But if you are gauging the whole class understanding and have no intention of going back over something that 85% of the class understands, then anonymity is the way to go.

Introducing CATS to your class

Tell students CATS are your "finger on the pulse" of student understanding – and you use CATS only to help you become a better instructor and to find those areas you need to re-explain. Once students realize you are not going to grade these assessments (usually), that they don't take much time, and you will actually use them to find out what needs to be re-explained, they are willing participants. However, if you keep doing CATS and never change anything – you lose their good will.

The Spirit of Creativity and Research

Formative techniques are fun because they embody the spirit of creativity and research. You are a detective trying to find out if students understand something without threatening them via grades. With this mission you can invent techniques appropriate to your subject material, audience, and style. There is nothing at all mysterious about this. The techniques on the next few pages include modifications of suggestions by Angelo and Cross and many other instructors who have "invented" and shared. College instructors around the world in one form or another are probably using these techniques whether or not they ever read a book on CATS. Experiment! Expect some CATS to work better one semester than another because classes are different. Don't throw them out. Try again, maybe with a better initial example and instructions. I still like to hand out slips of paper that include words and graphics for my CATS. It reinforces the instructions, gives me consistent sized pieces of paper to collect, and adds a bit of humor at times.

Classic Journalist's Summary

Angelo and Cross call this CAT the One Sentence Summary, but for some concepts you might have to stretch it to the Two Sentence Summary. It basically asks students to use an expanded set of classic journalism questions, the "Ws" and an "H": who? what? when? where? why? how? You give students the topic (a concept, not a fact) and the prompts – they write the summary sentence(s). Reproduce this CAT on half sheets of paper that students then turn in after a few volunteers share their responses in class. Read all the responses and thereby gauge the class understanding of the concept; make adjustments in teaching if necessary. This is a very effective technique and students like it – it stretches them. Time: about 2-3 minutes.

Journalist's Summary

In one or two sentences only, answer the questions about this topic: _____

Who?	Where?
What?	How?
When?	Why?

Theory into Practice and Theory into My Life

This is a very simple technique, but it is good at assessing higher order thinking skills at the application level. Introduce this technique verbally and go through an example or two on the board. If students cannot think of how the theory or concept you give them can be applied in "real life," then they probably do not understand it. You can narrow the parameters to fit your objectives, of course. "How could this be applied in geriatric nursing?" "How is this applied in the elementary math classroom?" "How is this applied during operant conditioning?" Time: 2 minutes.

Theory into My Life isn't for all types of classes, but it works beautifully in some subject areas (nursing, sales, business, psychology, HR, sociology and even technical classes). When students can apply a theory to their own life or the life of someone they know (and they are accurate), then they truly 'get it'. Adult learners really enjoy being acknowledged for their own level of experience, and they can come up with outstanding examples to share with the class.

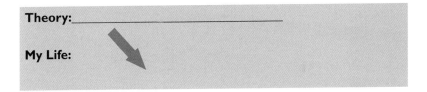

Connections to the Past

When students link new information to old information, they are more likely to remember it. This technique works well when you have made connections for students to previously covered material and want to make sure they understand and remember them. Again, the beauty of formative assessment is in its simplicity and the ease with which you can glance over the sheets for a holistic peek at how the whole class is doing. You are in charge of how detailed you want students to get and can establish the criteria within your verbal instructions. This is a tough CAT for a lot of students who are in the habit of just memorizing what is in front of them and not thinking about how it connects to anything! You will want to provide a couple examples. Time: depends upon topic, but 3-4 minutes. This one isn't easy.

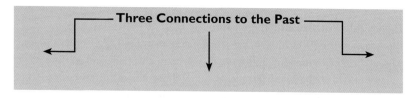

Connections Between Concepts

This one is a little easier for students, but it will reflect their understanding of the concepts and keep them actively engaged in thinking about the content you just presented.

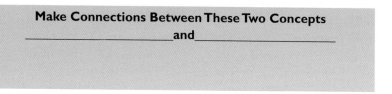

Draw and Label

In some subject areas you can tell at a glance if a subject is clear through the use of drawings or diagrams. If understanding a flow chart is important, you can provide the blank flow chart elements and have students label them.

The Defense Rests (Summarizing)

Having students summarize a process, a concept, or a theory is a good, solid technique of formative assessment. Of course, this is without notes, so information is strictly in their own words. I have tried this as a "closing argument," to give it a little "sizzle," depending upon the concept. Examples: Make a closing argument for using active learning in the classroom; make a closing argument for the presence of groupthink during the Bay of Pigs; make a closing argue for the influence of nature over nurture in brain development. If the "closing argument" doesn't fit your topic, come up with something else or just ask for a summary!

The Defense Rests

Indirect Formative Assessment

These formative techniques will not tell you what students have mastered but they will tell you their impressions of what confuses them or excites them. This is sometimes useful, especially if half the class is confused about the same thing. Obviously, you jump in then at the beginning of the next class and clarify. Again, if you do this at the end of class, you are likely to get a lot of mentions of the information that came last in your lecture as it is closest in time (recency effect). If you want that, great, but if you want students to think about the entire class period's worth of information, you may have to prod their memories with an outline on the PowerPoint.

What's still Confusing? (The Muddiest Point)

Whether you call this technique "The Muddiest Point" (Angelo and Cross) or find your own clever name relevant to your field (Black Hole for Today in Astronomy), this is about as direct as it gets when looking for points of confusion. Sometimes you get a lot of "nothing – I understood." This hopefully indicates teaching success. My only problem with Muddiest Point is that teachers overuse it. It is about the easiest formative assessment to use and students don't mind writing about their confusion. It's stress-free for them when anonymous. This is very popular for a reason, and you'll want to try it out.

Black Hole for Today
(or Muddiest Point?)
(or What's Still Confusing?)

Aha! Explained!

Students generally like this opportunity to talk briefly about an insight they had – an "aha." This is not a formative assessment to use every day because, let's face it, in even the best of classes not every day has an "aha" in it. But watch your class and keep your half-sheets ready. When you see "light bulbs" going off, you might want to capture a better understanding of what happened with an "Aha!" sheet.

This gives you clues about which of your examples connect with students and why something jelled for them (was it an image you used, a chart, a TED talk, a metaphor, an activity?). Monitor responses, though, for clarity of understanding.

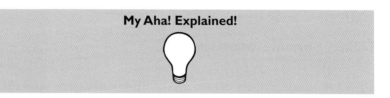

My Aha! Explained!

Exit Cards

Before students can leave for the day, they need to hand in an Exit Card (3x5 cardstock). You can come up with your own questions, but many teachers use some combination of these:

List 3 things you learned today
2 questions you wondered about
1 thing you are still confused about.

List the 3 most interesting things you heard today
2 activities that you felt helped you learn
1 way you can apply something you learned

Summative Direct Measures

You want to use variety in your summative direct assessments also. Don't use tests exclusively. Even in math, students can explain why they are doing what they are doing either in writing or orally, and they will benefit from that.

The most frequently used summative techniques are

- *Tests and Quizzes including (or not) a large Comprehensive Final Exam*
  Make sure you provide good review opportunities and maybe even broad study guides listing the big ideas/concepts any comprehensive test will cover.
- *Portfolios*
  Collected work from across the semester; student chooses contents. This is usually done once, but the work included covers the whole

semester. There is lots of information about how to structure portfolios and grade them on the internet.

- *Several Small Projects leading up to one large Final Project*

    As a summative assessment, a large final project should incorporate several major objectives of the course – example: three-dimensional mockup of an office sitting room, fully decorated, for an Interior Design class. The earlier projects then could have involved learning about the individual elements of the room like lighting, flooring choices, etc.

- *Laboratory Tasks*

    This may involve lab tests, lab reports, etc. all along the semester culminating in one large laboratory test involving tasks that demonstrate student skills, ability to analyze, etc.

- *Papers including a longer Final Paper*

    As a summative assessment, final papers should incorporate several major objectives of the class.

- *Presentations or Performances including Culminating Presentations* (solo or groups)

    Same theme here…a last presentation should be more complex, covering several major *objectives*. If a student gives three other presentations during the semester, they should be of lesser challenge and help build skills incrementally in preparation for the larger presentation.

- *Oral Exam*

    Used to be a favorite type of exam, one-on-one with the instructor, and is still the way college students are tested in much of Europe. An oral exam sums up a lot of information from objectives in several standard questions that are given to all students. Causes some anxiety and much studying; extremely useful and no cheating!

- *Journals*

    There are many different types of journals: self-reflective journals, current event application journals, analysis journals, critical thinking journals, and more. Usually students answer particular sets of questions provided by the instructor. Journals are usually turned in several times during the semester, and a final time at the end.

Of course, this list doesn't begin to catalog the full range of ways students can directly show you what they know during the semester. You can also try out:

Chapter questions	Case study analysis	Mind mapping
Debates	Test creation	PowerPoint Creation
Service Learning	Students Teaching	Article Review
Critiques	Panel Discussions	Field Trip Report
Peer Reviews	Create a video	Interview and Report
Create a study guide	Lead a discussion	Develop Instructions
Demonstrations	Research Project	Research Study Analysis

There is great benefit to having multiple ways of assessing student learning. First, not all students shine on tests or papers, but they'll amaze you with their video production or demonstrations covering the very same objectives. Second, variety in assessment honors the great diversity of people we have in our classes. College didn't used to do this. If you couldn't sit still and learn from a lecture and pass a midterm and final exam, well, you flunked out. A lot of clever, innovative people flunked out! Hopefully we are retaining a wider variety of thinking styles in our colleges today.

Remember that projects, papers, portfolios, presentations, etc. should have extremely clear criteria, given in writing. Students need to know exactly which outcomes they are responsible for mastering. They need to have the grading rubric in their hand while preparing so they know up front how their expertise will be judged. This goes for any summative component all along the semester.

Summative Indirect Measures

Your college performs most summative indirect measures: Program Reviews, course evaluations, graduation surveys, employer surveys, internship supervisor response items, etc. These measures help the college monitor general satisfaction and quality but certainly do not directly show student learning.

At the individual instructor level, you will not be developing many indirect summative measures with one exception: the detailed course evaluation. While the Research Office at your college will have a general course evaluation form for students to fill out every semester, it usually can't tell you much specific information that is actionable. In Skill #10, I discuss developing a summative indirect measure that will be more helpful.

Effective Tests and Test Banks

Most good textbooks come with test banks. Test banks are an incredible help. After all, they are usually developed by test item experts in the field of study, they have more items than you could ever sanely use, and the publishers have usually performed item analysis to ascertain which items are "hard" and "easy." And – let's face facts – all their essay items already have answers that you can make into handy rubrics for grading OR use as in-class activities! What a time saver! Test banks have a lot going for them, but we do have to use them mindfully.

Evaluate test banks carefully and choose the best items. Some test-bank items are too difficult and tricky – others are too low level, asking mainly knowledge questions at the "memorize these facts" level. Some have typos and incorrectly keyed items. The idea is to evaluate student learning on important areas in a field of study, not trivia specific to one textbook. Many test banks have their items keyed to Bloom's Taxonomy so you can choose items at all levels. This is a great feature.

- Another great feature is the ability to edit items. You can use the test bank as a base and change wording, etc. so items become your own and reflect your class content specifically.
- If the test bank has multiple choice items, see how many distracters questions have. Five distracters make multiple choice questions quite a bit harder for students and harder for you to edit and make them your own.
- Never "random select" test bank items when making a test; carefully match items to your objectives. If you test on-line, choose 3–4 similar items on each objective, load them all up into your LMS and then randomize from there so students have slightly different tests. (IT will help you do this.)
- Test frequently – over each chapter, if possible, or once every two weeks. Students will learn more with smaller chunks to remember and be less anxious about testing. "Midterms" and "Finals" as the sole tests are simply unacceptable. I feel four tests in a course like Anatomy is also unacceptable. There is just too much information and students will cram rather than remember. *Frequent testing* is the best practice if you want students to remember more!
- Incorporating a comprehensive final exam pulling from your chapter tests is a good idea. If you structure it correctly, you have the opportunity to correlate sections with your objectives for the course and see which were fully understood by the majority and which may need some teaching tune-up next semester.

- Give adequate time to students taking tests. Some are slower readers.
- Do not mix the chronological sequence of material, if possible; keep the book order.
- Continually pull in important points from previous tests all along the semester to help students process this info into their long term memory.
- Give students item variety on tests. Include multiple choice, essay, short answer, etc. Variety is good!
- It is nice if you have a few "extra" items on each test, allowing students to choose 25 of 30, or 40 of 45. This actually relaxes students a great deal as they feel slightly more in control of the situation. Instructors frequently use this option with essay items (*Choose three of the above five questions*) but somehow forget they can do this with other formats just as easily. It works well.

Developing Your Own Test Items

Glutton for Punishment???? Develop all your own tests!

Despite the many advantages of test banks, many instructors want to develop their own tests. Fine. The web and your college library have resources that can tell you how to create good items. Test design is a very specialized field and isn't the objective of this book. Developing good test items isn't as easy as it looks, and I've seen many otherwise good instructors create really bad multiple choice or essay items! But here are a few tips overall:

- Don't use all one type of question item
- Design some items for higher levels of Bloom than knowledge
- Match items to your objectives
- Have enough items to cover the content (and enough exams overall)
- Make sure items are crystal clear
- Take into consideration your own limitations: a 400 student lecture class is probably not the best place to use essay items, even when they might be the best format to test the complexity you desire. Reality sets in. We don't always get the test format we crave. We need to provide prompt feedback to students if a test is to serve as a learning opportunity, not just a grading opportunity. Four hundred essay tests will not have a fast turnaround.

True/False

- First, ask yourself if these are worth developing. Will they really test student understanding? Will they cover enough information? Can you get enough depth into them? (Hard to do!)

- Make sure you cover major points, not insignificant items.
- Avoid "all" "always" "never" as these are clues that the item is likely False.
- Have students convert all false statements into true statements in order to get points – this helps eliminate the guessing that is so easy with true/false.
- Don't use negatives/double negatives, which create a lack of clarity for the reader.
- Be sure only one major point is covered per item.
- Be sure your item is honestly unequivocally either True or False (harder to achieve than it looks).

Matching

- Again, ask yourself if these are worthwhile. Many matching tests are simple recognition. Is this enough for you? (Depends on the goal.)
- Note…a ten-point matching quiz that IS simple recognition at the beginning of each class session can sure help assure students read. Matching items at this level are easy to make up, too, and Word tables make tests easy to produce.
- You can make matching more challenging by having extra items on the response side or allow answers to be used more than once.
- Matching items can be at the understanding and application levels too. Use mini scenarios. On one side, stage a brief scenario in one or two sentences. Then students must match them up to the theory or the term they represent, or even the correct treatment. When you get into these brief scenarios the matching test becomes quite an interesting and versatile format.

Essays

- If you are only looking for facts, use a different test form. Essay tests are best when you want evaluation, synthesis, analysis, application…based upon knowledge and understanding.
- Create your answers as you create your test items. If the answers are not straightforward or become long and convoluted, then your essay item has multiple interpretations. Reword for clarity or avoid.
- If students are going to hand-write, try out your essay items yourself, by hand, to see how long your test takes to answer, then add a whole lot of extra minutes.
- Some instructors give a choice of essay items (answer 4 of 5) but making sure each item is "equal" in difficulty level is hard and some test experts feel this is actually giving different tests. I see their point. You'll have to weight the pros and cons. A history instructor I know who wrote excellent essay items always gave a list of the potential questions to students beforehand. They had the

opportunity to study all the items though they knew only a selection would appear on the test. Another idea to ponder.

- Essays cover less content so you will want to combine them with other test item types to make sure you test your students over a wide range of information/knowledge.
- Try "mini" essays – a cross between the essay and the "long" short answer for part of the test.
- Teach your students how you want them to answer an essay item before you use them on a test. Do you want them to have a real "intro, body, conclusion"? Don't assume they learned this in high school. Show them how to read essay items and pick out the words that should guide their answer like "compare and contrast" "the three main reasons" "two primary regulations that…".
- Decide if spelling and grammar are going to count and tell your students ahead of time. If an answer is correct but absolutely horribly written, how many points do you take off? Obviously, this will vary with subject area, but it bears consideration.
- Essay items are easy to write poorly.

Multiple-Choice

It's so easy to write bad multiple choice items. Are you really sure you want to go here? It may be better to use the test bank and adapt some of their items with your own twist. But if you insist – there are whole books written on this topic – consult one!

> **You should develop your own multiple choice items only**
> a.   cows come home
> b.   after you have read and understood a good book on multiple choice item development
> c.   you are short for time
> d.   you know how to really develop good true/false items
> e.   you are a great teacher
>
> Ooh…that's a GOOD example of a really BAD multiple choice test item!

The Multi-layered Scenario/Case Study Test Format

An excellent testing method is the scenario/case study with multiple questions asked after it. You can write up a brief paragraph that allows you to present a case study or a scenario in such a way that multiple questions can be asked in different formats. In the first example that follows, there are short answer, essay, and fill-in-the-blank items, and multiple choice could very easily be added. By the time students are done answering this test item, the instructor will have an excellent idea about what aspects of research design they understand.

In the second example, charts are the focal point. In many fields, being able to understand, interpret, and develop clear graphical representations of data is important. Again, this type of testing is challenging and requires a great deal more than memorization. That's a good thing! Students will be showing how they interpret charts and if they understand aspects of research design such as which studies can show cause and effect and what a correlation represents.

If you take the time to create these types of tests, you will want to protect them. You don't want these out floating around in student circles, or you find students do better each semester. You will also want to let students practice on samples as this is quite a different format than most of them are used to.

A Scenario Test Example

Psychologist Jan Beyer wants to test whether an anti-anxiety drug or cognitive behavioral therapy will work best for teens who have serious social anxiety at school. A large school system in a major city is willing to work with her. The schools are scattered throughout the city. Through various sources, they have signed up 100 sophomore-level students (70 girls, 30 boys) whose parents will allow them to participate, including students at an all-girls charter school. Jan divides the group of 100 into three groups: one will be the Control Group, one will be the anti-anxiety drug group, and one will get cognitive behavioral therapy (CBT). Because of the problems of transportation, she uses all student volunteers in School A for the Control, School B for the drug, and School C for the CBT. She has the school counselor at School C run the individual CBT training sessions, which are held once a week for four weeks. The Control Group gets to watch a relaxing movie together once a week. The Drug Group is given an appropriate dose of drugs during the four weeks. Three students drop out of that group because they had a bad reaction to the drug. At the end of the four weeks all participants take the same anxiety paper and pencil test that they took at the beginning. Jan is surprised because the Control Group actually improved more than either of the treatment groups. That wasn't what she was expecting at all.

1. What was the independent variable? Why?
2. What was the dependent variable? Why?
3. Was the sampling sound, or could something be improved?
4. What do you think of assignment to groups? Was it sound, or could something be improved?
5. How was social anxiety operationalized?
6. Did Jan control everything she should have controlled?
7. What are some potential confounding variables?
8. Can the study results be generalized? Why or why not?
9. This type of study is the only type that can show_____and _____.
10. Redesign this study to include improvements you feel should be made.

The Chart Scenario Example

Professor Garend Touffell is interested in poverty and reading readiness [measured as phonological awareness]. Working with the local school system, he was able to get income, race, and preschool screening data without names attached for all three elementary schools in a midwestern town of 20,000. In total, he has information and scores for 3,400 children, collected by the schools for a period of 10 years. The charts he developed with his data are shown below. Answer the following questions:

What does the correlation between income and phonological awareness actually show? (select all that are correct)

❑ As income goes up, phonological awareness goes down – a negative correlation
❑ As income goes down, phonological awareness goes down – a negative correlation
❑ As income goes up, phonological awareness goes up – a positive correlation
❑ As income goes down, phonological awareness goes up – a negative correlation
❑ As income goes down, phonological awareness goes down – a positive correlation
❑ That income and phonological awareness have a positive correlational relationship
❑ That income and phonological awareness have a negative correlational relationship
❑ Race impacts phonological awareness
❑ Early daycare impacts phonological awareness

Explain in brief essay form:

1. Can Professor Touffell conclude that poverty causes a drop in phonological awareness? Why or why not?

2. Can Professor Touffell conclude that race causes a drop in phonological awareness? Why or why not?

3. Can Professor Touffell conclude that early daycare education is connected to a drop in phonological awareness? Why or why not?

4. Reread Professor Touffell's conclusion. Do you feel his conclusion was justified by the data? Why or why not?

5. Could there be a different interpretation or explanation from the same data? Explain.

Skill 8:

GRADING: BE FAIR, BE TRANSPARENT

Students know you are going to evaluate their work. They just ask that you be fair and transparent.

Grading Scales

- Be sure to check if your college has a recommended (or required) grading scale.
- Check with other instructors to see if there is an "unofficial" grading scale agreement among them. You do not want your scale vastly higher or lower than other faculty teaching the same class.
- Remember: A few points make a big difference to students.
- Think about your scale: should a student still pass a course if they know only 60% of the material? Would you want that engineer to design a bridge you drive over?

Privacy

Of course, if you just post grades on-line inside the LMS all the issues below are a moot point! Take the time to learn how to use the grade book on-line. It saves you a lot of hassle and, in the end, time. But if you really want to go paper instead of technology, you have to be careful about student privacy.

- You cannot post scores on your office door or outside your classroom using student names, even just their last names, their SSN, or their student ID.
- You cannot pass a list of grades around class with the above information on it either.
- If a parent calls and wants to know how a student is doing, you cannot tell them if the student is over 18, unless the student has signed a special waiver and you have seen it.
- Do not give papers back to anyone besides the student. Roommates cannot pick up their friends' grades or papers for them.
- Check with your department to see if you can assign random numbers to students and post grades publically using them. Rules may differ.

Fairness in Grading

- You must maintain fairness. If you let one student make up a quiz for "x" reason, you'll need to make that quiz available for all students with reasons equal to "x", and when you think it through how do you really know "x" is true? Then you get in the messy arena of deciding what a "worthy excuse" is. *How many times has your grandmother died?* I recommend dropping the lowest two or three quiz scores and not allowing "make-ups" except for doctor or military excuses. This cuts out a lot of uncomfortable decision-making and angst on your part.
- If you give one student an extra credit opportunity because they begged so hard for anything to raise their grade you finally caved in – then you absolutely have to offer that extra credit opportunity to everyone else too.
- Beware the Halo Effect. This is where a student wears "a halo" – either a shiny or a tarnished one. We are human and cannot avoid giving some students the benefit of the doubt (we want their papers to be good because they are so nice!) and others the opposite. You need to develop methods to control the Halo Effect. On-line, where papers are submitted into a drop-box system, you will always know who submitted what unless some clever IT person has already developed a system of anonymity. With paper products, have students write an assigned number, not their name, on the back of all papers, so you don't know whose you are grading. An imperfect system, but it helps.
- Do not always collect essay tests in the same order. Have written criteria for right answers. Don't grade essays all at once in a marathon session or when you are already exhausted. The first and last essays will likely get a different reading if you do. This is good practice with a stack of papers too.

- Strive to have as many objectively graded projects/tests as possible in each class. This way your own subjective feelings won't be a liability.
- Avoid the impression of subjective grading on your more "subjective" projects by using a good, sound, grading rubric that breaks down the key grading criteria fully for students. Give this rubric to students as they are preparing their papers or projects – don't keep grading rubrics secret.
- Keep good records. Believe me, at some point in your career you'll have to justify a grade.

Grade Inflation

Do you want to be known as the instructor to take for the "Easy A?" Probably not. But creeping grade inflation, especially in courses with subjective projects, is sometimes a problem. You want to be known as fair, not easy, so be sure to set your standards high enough to differentiate between students who really do know the material at the "A" level and those who do not. Should you adopt a bell curve in your grading? If you are doing good active teaching with multiple opportunities for students to rehearse and over-learn, most of your students should not be earning "C" grades. But it is also a rare college class indeed where the majority earn "A" grades at the undergraduate level. If your classes are over-loaded with "A" and "B" grades and you have very few "C" and "D" grades, look at your standards and graded assignments. Are you offering too many easy point opportunities that aren't really reflective of college level work? Can you really discriminate between those who put forth the effort to study and under-stand the material and those who don't?

People earn their own "F" or "D" or "C"– assign it. People EARN grades; you don't GIVE them. You just add up the points they earned and match that against your grading scale. (Or hit the button and the on-line system adds it all up for you.) Watch how you talk about grades. Many of us have the tendency to say *"I Gave…."* You did not. The student EARNED that grade.

Grading Discussion

Grading discussion is challenging, and you will want to experiment. Discussion points can be contentious because if you don't track who is talking at the time they talk, you are grading later on "general impressions," and memory, frankly, isn't that accurate. It is influenced by the halo effect. Some instructors mark down each time a student participates on a check sheet, but you have to know your students' names well, of course, and marking can be time consuming. A full room of students makes this harder. You can ask students to self-grade and then compare their impressions with yours. Self-grading with a small rubric can help. Something as simple as

Circle answers for items 1 and 2. – Add your total and reflect on ways to improve. Name_____			
1. Amount:	0 Oops	1 I contributed once	2 I contributed twice	3 I contributed three or four times, no more
2. Quality:	0 = talked too much, not at all, or didn't add anything new 1 = made mainly new points 2= made new points and asked others good questions		
Total for Today: _____ Ways I can improve discussion for next class:_____			

One clever Communications instructor we knew made little rubber-banded bundles of 3 flat sticks for each student with their names on them. Students picked them up from the back table when they came to class. As discussion went on, the instructor would collect a stick from a student who made a worthwhile comment and put it in a can labeled "Points" that she carried around with her. If the comment was just "I agree with Suzie" she didn't collect the stick. Comments had to add to the discussion in a meaningful way. Some students complained it was "babyish" at the beginning of each semester, but by class evaluation time she was always praised for the system and how it created great discussions. More students talked. The benefits were tangible. And in her class, you could make only three contributions per discussion period. When your sticks were gone, you were mute. So students who had a tendency to take over thought more about which comments they wanted to make. At the end of class, attendance was easy – which bundles were left on the back table? And points were also easy. Whose sticks were in the can labeled "Points"? When giving discussion participation points, you must come up with an objective way to tally them up and put this into the syllabus. This clever system certainly worked.

Grading In-Class Activities

If you give points for in-class activities, use criteria for doling them out. Don't give full points for "doing" the activity. There should be a point difference between barely participating while sitting silently in a group and actively jumping in, asking challenging questions, and discussing fully. It's useful on several levels to have students grade themselves for group activities, and it can help shape their behavior as they have the criteria for good participation in front of them every class day. Here are two ways to help shape group behaviors:

Rate Yourself on Your Activity Participation Today
Date:_____ Name:_____ Activity:_____
Circle points

I was here, but barely breathing; what was the activity? OR I think I dominated and didn't give others time to think before I talked again.	Breathing was steady, but I didn't actively contribute much to group; listened every now and then	I was a little engaged and helped answer the questions a few times; was listening much of the time	I was more engaged, helped answer most questions & asked questions; listened most of the time	Really engaged, helped answer questions, asked my group questions too; helped keep us on track; encouraged others to talk; carefully listened to others
1	2	3	4	5

Points Your Group Members would Probably Agree to Give You?_____

Rate Yourself on Your Group Activity Participation Today Date:_____
Name_____ **Circle what applies; answer the questions**
Group Members: _____

1. How well was I prepared:

Didn't	Read Part	Read Most	Read All	Read All, took notes

2. How many times did I contribute something that helped us answer the questions?

Didn't, Kept Quiet	Once	Twice	3+ Times	Oops may have actually talked too much

3. Did I help my Group stay on the Topic?		
No	Tried to keep us focused, yes	Oops, may have gotten off topic myself too much

4. Did I stay engaged with the group discussion?			
No	A little	Fairly engaged	Really was in there, fully engaged

5. I give myself _____ out of 5 points for my contribution to the group success today.
My group would probably give me _____ out of 5 points.

6. What I'll do to improve:

Fairly Evaluate Group Work

Some people hate group projects. No, "hate" is too mild a word. Some people absolutely LOATHE group projects. Why? Sometimes people are just shy, but usually it is because the *grading never seems fair*. The group members who want an "A" end up doing most of the work, and group members who hardly participate at all get to slide along for the ride and end up with a grade they don't deserve in the end. This happens across the grade spectrum, including graduate school. So how can you fairly evaluate group work?

First: set the project up for fairness to begin with

- Address the issues inherent in group work when you introduce the project. Discuss the "perfect" group and the truly "dysfunctional" group. Talk about what expectations group members have for one another and how they can head off (or report) problems. Make the consequences for being a sluggard obvious. Some instructors allow groups to "fire" members at certain points in the process.
- Have a list of tasks that will need to be done and written expectations for each. Individuals should sign on the dotted line, literally, to say they understand how to participate. Group members need to know clearly what is expected of them.
- Set a minimum number of meetings acceptable.
- You might have individual group members submit journal entries from each meeting summarizing their own input and the meeting. Have these turned

in during the developing project, usually weekly or bi-weekly, not just at the end. Have them worth points.

- When the project is introduced, hand students the rubric you will use to evaluate their project and the final rubric they will use to evaluate the contribution of each member. Particularly on the latter rubric, make the criteria behavioral in nature so group members do not have to give a holistic grade, but rather they can address how many times someone came to meetings, contributed resources, delivered their part on time, and worked. Of course you also want to include group skills like *listened to others' ideas, was flexible, didn't take over,* etc. But the bulk of the rubric should not be impressions.
- Consider dividing the project grade into a combination of individual and group contribution points. Example: Individual paper but group presentation.
- If the project involves a presentation and you want every member speaking rather than just the brave, polished one, make this clear ahead of time and put it on your grading rubric.
- Give some time during class for groups to coordinate. Find out if half your class commutes or works. College is not peopled with residential students with time on their hands anymore. Don't just assign a group project and expect everyone to have time to get together a lot. It is a true burden for working, commuting parents and students who work or drive long hours to get together with a group five times.
- Set up group areas in the LMS for your class where students can "meet."
- Realize that some people are just learning to function within a group. Give guidance and help along the way. Don't expect students to already know how to do this well. Most members will be unskilled to one degree or another at handling group dynamics. You may want to tap a faculty member who teaches Small Group Communication to come do a 20-minute lesson on functioning well during a group project. Ask around.

Second: use evaluation forms for all group members repeatedly

Periodically throughout the project (starting early) pass out individual evaluations of progress in class without warning. Don't let people talk while they fill them out. You will be able to see some students gasp. They didn't attend any meetings and hardly know who is in their group. This is rather motivating to *get with the program.* These evaluations can be worth points too, but let the first one serve as a motivational warning, not an assessment. When you look over these progress forms, you'll be able to see if group members have the same perspective and intervene if a group is really having problems. Remember, you are helping them build a skill that many did not come to college with.

My Name:_____		Topic of our Project:_____	
How many meetings has your group had so far?_____		How many did you attend?_____	
What resources did you bring to the meeting(s)?_____			
Who else attended?	# of times	What resources did they bring?	Where is your group in the process so far?
_____ _____ _____	_____ _____ _____	_____ _____	

Peer and Self-Evaluation

Whether you are designing a peer evaluation instrument to be used on a group project or for students to evaluate a classmate's speech, the bulk of items need to be behavioral in nature to avoid points being deducted for personality clashes or popularity. By behavioral I mean students can literally see, hear, measure, count, the behavior. Think in terms of how useful the feedback will be to students. *"They all liked me"* is certainly fun feedback, but *"Didn't always show up on time to meetings"* or *"Rarely looked at audience"* tells students what needs adjusting in the future. This is much more useful.

You may want final peer evaluations filled out in class unless groups were so big this would take up way too much time. Students should receive points for filling them out completely and thoughtfully. I do not recommend using solely peer evaluations to assign a grade. They should count for some smaller percentage of the total grade, though, for both evaluators and the evaluated. You will want to read through the evaluations from individual groups all at once and see if they have a measure of agreement about what went on. It's a personal instructor choice whether or not you turn peer evaluations over to students at the end of the semester or just provide them with a summary. But if you choose to turn them back make sure evaluator names are not left on the evaluations. Whether you will be turning them back or not needs to also be in the syllabus. This is a time when creating a one-minute video per student is helpful to all (with a laptop and free software, very easily done). You can summarize the peer input, telling them what their strengths appeared to be and what it seems they could improve upon. Email the video. Feedback given. Little potential for fallout to peers in their group.

Self-evaluations should follow the same guidelines except they also include several questions about the process, time management, and metacognition. In both peer and self-evaluations, you are trying to shape behaviors. Those are the items that should be on the instruments; the tool itself becomes a teaching activity. On self-evaluations, self reflection about lessons learned, barriers, overcoming barriers, assumptions, etc. help students think and grow. Always make sure students receive peer and self-evaluation forms before their projects begin so they clearly know the target behaviors you expect.

Computing a Group Grade

Coming up with a final grade for a group project is a learning experience for the instructor, too. Does everyone get the same grade? Do you grade each section presented by a different person individually? Or do you divide the grading into 20% for the individual section presented, 20% for the overall group effort, 10% from group peers, 10% self-evaluation, and 40% for an individual paper on the project? What if you asked for a group paper? What then? There are numerous ways to actually arrive at the final grade, but it is certainly best to think through each scenario carefully before making a decision. And you will need clear guidelines for every aspect you are going to grade.

What is fair? Students, of course, have some ideas on this topic. First, it's important you help them understand why a group project will accomplish some of the course objectives. If teams are part of workplace reality in your field, then you probably have an objective for teamwork. That makes an easy sell. Turn students loose to come up with a way to grade group projects that they feel is fair, sensible, and actually doable. You don't have to adopt it 100% but consider meshing parts with your own ideas.

Consider having group members write individual reflective papers at the close of the project evaluating what they learned, what went well, how they felt the grading process is working, what barriers arose in the group process and how these could be avoided or diminished in future group projects. These papers should be part of the points for their own grade. Guide their reflection with a set of questions to answer including metacognition items (thinking about their own thinking). These reflections will be invaluable to you as you refine your abilities to design and evaluate group projects fairly.

Skill 9:

MASTER THE GRADING RUBRIC

When you have something to grade that is more subjective (you personally have to make a quality judgment) than objective (hard cold test items), you need a scoring scheme. Instructors always have a guide to judge the quality of student work in their heads, but assessment accountability and good educational principles demand that you also have it on paper. Rubrics to the rescue! A good grading rubric will save you time and hassles when grading and provides a target for students to aim at. Good rubrics are excellent learning/teaching tools.

Rubrics seem so easy to develop – which means they are easy to develop badly! A good rubric takes time and lots of serious thought, but once a good rubric is done it can usually be used time and time again with only minor revisions. Don't let developing rubrics make you nervous, however. You create them all the time mentally. Think about purchasing a dozen baking potatoes. You have some criteria in your head for baking potatoes: use a Russet, good size, not many eyes, certainly no sprouts, no green spots, no mushy spots, etc. These are your basic criteria: type, size, blemishes, etc. When you look through a stack of potatoes to pick 12, you look them over and grade them on how closely they match your perfect criteria. Some do, some almost do, some you toss aside. You have a rubric in your head!

It's important to realize that rubrics are in a perpetual state of minor improvement. You think you have one just right and then while you use it to grade a stack of project summaries you notice all the problems. Back to the drawing board for next semester. I don't think I have ever designed a rubric that I didn't want to improve. But this is fun, in a strange way. It assures you are continually thinking!

The Basic Rubric

You may be familiar with the most basic skeleton of rubrics:

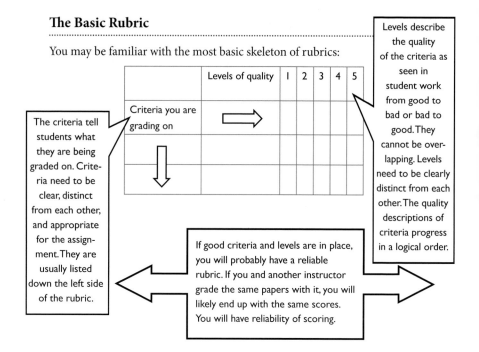

The criteria tell students what they are being graded on. Criteria need to be clear, distinct from each other, and appropriate for the assignment. They are usually listed down the left side of the rubric.

Levels describe the quality of the criteria as seen in student work from good to bad or bad to good. They cannot be overlapping. Levels need to be clearly distinct from each other. The quality descriptions of criteria progress in a logical order.

If good criteria and levels are in place, you will probably have a reliable rubric. If you and another instructor grade the same papers with it, you will likely end up with the same scores. You will have reliability of scoring.

Good Criteria on a Very Basic Rubric

- Focus on the major components of the project being graded
  - ° You must be able to identify the essence, the components of your desired outcome in detail – these are the criteria you are grading on.
  - ° The criteria you identify should be fairly equal in importance
- Use the professional language of your field (but teach students what these words mean first)
- Stay so clear everyone in class can understand them. No fuzzy or ambiguous language. (*Smells good* is ambiguous language.)

Good Quality Levels on a Very Basic Rubric

- Have the right number of levels to differentiate student work into sensible quality divisions
  - ° Too many levels force you into arbitrary quality decisions (Bad, Poor, Average -, Average, Good, Good +, Excellent, Super Excellent???) You'll be screaming.
  - ° Too few levels don't make sense or have huge quality leaps between them (Poor, Average, Terrific) and add in some scoring/points complexity you don't need.

- You might consider a 1 – 5 scale because this equates to the A – F scale students are so familiar with. But you have to see if you can actually manage to create five different shades of quality before using it. You might find a 1 – 4 scale better for your situation.
- Have a clear description for each level of quality
  - They provide guides for students as to what you expect of an "A" or "5" paper, a "B" or "4" paper, etc.
  - These provide a means of enhancing reliability. Two raters looking at the same essay, paper, presentation, or portfolio, should be able to come up with the same score if the descriptions are clearly written. Without a description for each quality level, this is highly unlikely to happen. What is a "2" performance on a typical 1 – 4 rubric scale? It doesn't mean the same to everyone if there isn't a clear description of "2."

Typical Problems with Basic Rubrics

- Don't have quality levels fully described, they just put 1 – 5 as headings on blank cells
- Have too many quality categories – how do you grade spelling on a 1 – 10 scale?
- Include too many items or concepts in a single criteria cell. If a single criteria lists six things, what do you do if the student includes all but one? All but two?
- Don't have criteria with equal weight, or leave some real essentials out
- Break down the criteria into way too many little components so the rubric goes on for pages
- Don't carry the same criteria or components across all the quality categories
- Have overlapping levels of quality

Example Basic Rubric

First, identify the major components or criteria you'll be grading on — the essentials — with approximately equal importance to the success of the project.

Second, decide how many quality levels make sense. This may change as you actually write your descriptions and find some items don't fit your scheme. Then you'll have to revise. Remember, rubrics take some time! We are used to 5 pts (A, B, C, D, F) but those shades of gray are very difficult to create across some criteria. Four quality levels are easier. You can have two sections on your rubric, with different scales, one longer, one shorter — just separate them and anchor them individually and make sure the math works out. Nothing says you can't have a three level rubric with scores at 1, 3, and 5 points. Can you give decimal points for something "between average and good?" Sure. It's your rubric.

Third, decide on the aspects you'll be judging for each component. Don't get too complex. As you teach additional aspects during the semester, add them in to your rubrics. When developing a rubric, it is useful to start with the "A" product. Much easier to think about this way. Then move backwards toward the lowest level of quality.

Fourth, *make certain you carry the same identical aspects across all the quality categories. If you mention "clarity" under any category, then it has to be mentioned under all categories. You don't have to use identical words, however. Do not add in elements in one category that aren't judged in the others.*

Note: lots of rubrics have more than one "subcriteria" in each cell. But that means you are making a judgment call again. What if the voice was heard, the presenter knew her material cold and had no notes, but didn't step out into the audience? What do you do? Take something like ½ a point off? These are all issues worth thinking about and there are ways to fix this one — see the next example.

Three Minute Term Explanation Criteria	Needs Significant Improvement 1	Needs Improvement 2	Average 3	Good 4	Excellent 5
Organization	Presentation seemed unorganized and hard to follow. Lack of **clarity** confused audience.	Organization lacked logical progression in several places; **unclear** several times. Not easy to follow along consistently	Some parts easy to follow, but wondered where we were going a couple times; organization a little **unclear** in places.	Mostly easy to follow; mainly well organized; minimal issues with **clarity** and logical sequencing	Very easy to follow; thoughtfully organized, **clear** and logically sequenced throughout
Accuracy					Content was 100% accurate; all facts referenced; sources reliable
Presentation Style					Voice is easily heard; knew material so looked at audience instead of notes; came out from behind podium and into audience

Refined Rubric with Sub-criteria Points

The rubric below is a favorite with many instructors. It beautifully handles the problem of multiple subcriteria in a cell. The example is for a beginning essay in English Composition. Each box is worth points within each cell.

Major Components of Essay #1	0 pts each ❑ Needs significant improvement or missing altogether	I pt each ❑ Needs some improvement before it is acceptable	2 pts each ❑ Acceptable	3 pts each ❑ Good - shows good control over this aspect
Introduction	❑ **Thesis** missing or not understandable; ❑ Reader is probably **confused**; several sentences don't make sense ❑ No **hook** evident at all	❑ **Thesis** might confuse or mis-lead reader; ❑ Some sentences **confuse** or off target; ❑ Lacks a suf-ficient **hook** to intrigue reader	❑ **Thesis** there but not laser clear; ❑ One sentence a bit **confusing;** ❑ Not quite as **hooking** (might lack examples/appeal)	❑ Clear **thesis;** we have a target ❑ No **confus-ing** sentences; ❑ **Hooks** reader rapidly and all
Body				*Notice the 3 main qualities of a good Introduction are carefully carried across all levels.*
Conclusion				
Spelling, Grammar, Syntax				
Coherence				
Unity				

This type of rubric solves the issue of multiple subcriteria in a cell. You might have someone who wrote a clear Thesis and had only one Confusing Sentence but no hook at all. How many points would they earn for their Introduction? This system works very well. The use of checkboxes beside each individual subcriteria allows the instructor to provide an enormous amount of feedback to students without having to hand write the same thing over and over.

As students become familiar with more information during the semester, rubrics should change and include more elements. You should not be using the same rubric to grade the first paper and the final paper or the first machined part and the final machined part. You expect students to master new skills all semester and you should add those in to your rubrics along the way. For instance, in machine tool classes, tolerance levels are critical. But at the beginning, be a bit more lenient on being "off." As class progresses and skills are building, get stricter and stricter. By the time a student graduates she/he should be able to machine parts within tolerance levels demanded by industry. But if you started grading them like that at the beginning you might scare off your entire student body! Your rubrics should reflect the idea that students are learning a skill set step-by-step, not that students arrived with that skill set already intact.

Grading Rubric for Individual Comments with Weighted Cells

Some instructors want to write comments on student work. This rubric combines the benefits of individual written comments with the structure of a rubric. It is easily adapted to many subject areas. Note that each row's weight in the overall grade is not identical. Weighting is useful because some elements are more important than others, yet you want students to be aware they need *all* elements for a good, complete project.

[Sample here includes only a few components of the original rubric.]

Rubric with points already weighted in cells

Component	Not Here	Attempt made, but still needs polish and consistency	Adequate; shows understanding but not full control yet	Well done; shows clear control in this area	Your Points out of Possible Points
Clear thesis statement in opening paragraph: clarity and purpose	0	*I think I know which sentence your thesis is – I'm not positive* 2	4	6	2/6
Opening "hooks" reader: we have an idea why this is important	0	1	2	*Very interesting hook. I definitely am intrigued.* 3	3/3

The "I Have No Time At ALL" Checklist Rubric

Face facts. Full rubrics take development time. Sometimes you don't have time. Should you forget the rubric idea completely? No. Please don't go back to having your grading criteria all in your head, which makes grading seem very subjective. Instead, use a "checklist" rubric. They are fast to develop and will still help students receive lots of feedback. They aren't as reliable as a full rubric, of course, but they will still help you be more objective while grading. When you have more time, develop a full rubric and retire the checklist. (See example on page 132)

Headers on Rubrics

You gave your students guidelines for their paper or project. What do you do with a paper that gets turned in and reads well but doesn't meet the full set of guidelines you communicated? What if Joe's paper has everything except academic references and the whole purpose of the assignment was to do academic research? If you have points on your grading rubric for the references, Joe will get 0 in that cell, but he'll still pass, maybe with an excellent grade. This causes a lot of gnashing of teeth for instructors (and inevitable rubric revision).

To avoid this problem try adding a "header" on the top of your rubrics. Headers illuminate the guidelines. Pass your grading rubric out with the syllabus or at least way before the project due date. The "header" will help students stay on track and the rubric will shape their skills. Certainly they should have no questions about why they received an F grade if they turned in two pages when you clearly (and in writing!) asked for five.

Now, of course, you need to follow through and do what you say. Don't grade papers that don't meet the requirements if you say you won't. Many students will be floored you are actually going to do this, so start with a smaller gentler version of your header for the first paper or project and allow students to resubmit for full points in one week. This gets students used to actually meeting the parameters of the header. Many students are not used to being held accountable for completing an assignment as it was assigned. But it might be nice to wean them early into actually doing their work according to instructions. Headers actually improve the quality of papers many instructors receive. (See example on page 133)

Final Paper Criteria – English Composition I (Particular attention was paid to items in Bold)

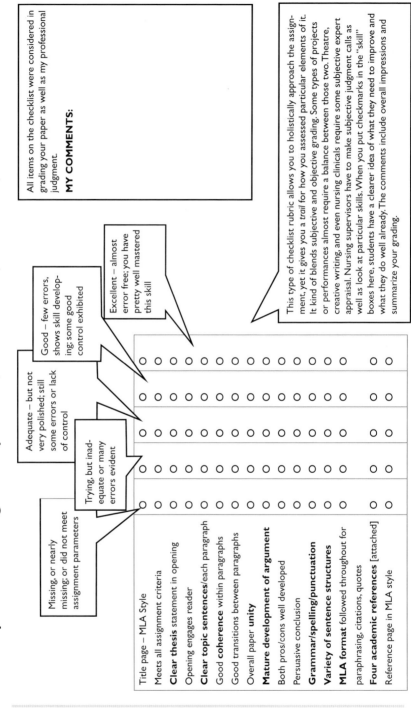

All items on the checklist were considered in grading your paper as well as my professional judgment.

MY COMMENTS:

Missing, or nearly missing; or did not meet assignment parameters

Trying, but inadequate or many errors evident

Adequate – but not very polished; still some errors or lack of control

Good – few errors, shows skill developing; some good control exhibited

Excellent – almost error free; you have pretty well mastered this skill

Title page – MLA Style
Meets all assignment criteria
Clear thesis statement in opening
Opening engages reader
Clear topic sentences/each paragraph
Good **coherence** within paragraphs
Good transitions between paragraphs
Overall paper **unity**
Mature development of argument
Both pros/cons well developed
Persuasive conclusion
Grammar/spelling/punctuation
Variety of sentence structures
MLA format followed throughout for paraphrasing, citations, quotes
Four academic references [attached]
Reference page in MLA style

This type of checklist rubric allows you to holistically approach the assignment, yet it gives you a *trail* for how you assessed particular elements of it. It kind of blends subjective and objective grading. Some types of projects or performances almost require a balance between those two. Theatre, creative writing, and even nursing clinicals require some subjective expert appraisal. Nursing supervisors have to make subjective judgment calls as well as look at particular skills. When you put checkmarks in the "skill" boxes here, students have a clearer idea of what they need to improve and what they do well already. The comments include overall impressions and summarize your grading.

Research Paper [only the header to the full rubric is shown here]
This rubric will be used to grade your paper, but in order for me to even start grading <u>all</u> the following parameters must be met.
Check off each box before you turn your paper in and sign that you have fulfilled these basic requirements.

1 – Typed, 12-font, 1-inch margins, double-spaced, stapled, and *turned in on time*
    ❑   Yes (continue with grading)
    ❑   No (stop grading here)
2 – Right *number* (five) and *types* of references used [academic: web, book, journal, interview] clearly cited on a Works Cited page
    ❑   Yes (continue with grading)
    ❑   No (stop grading here)
3 – Copies of source document quotes are attached AND areas quoted or paraphrased *highlighted*
    ❑   Yes (continue with grading)
    ❑   No (stop grading here)
4 – MLA Format used throughout including title page and Works Cited
    ❑   Yes (continue with grading)
    ❑   No (stop grading here)
5 – Length: *over* five pages long, *excluding* title page and Works Cited page
    ❑   Yes (continue with grading)
    ❑   No (stop grading here)

I have fulfilled the basic requirements:_____

Skill 10:

PLAN FOR CONTINUAL IMPROVEMENT

Excellent teachers generally have an improvement mindset and they are right to have one. Generally, everything *can* be improved. Teaching is a shifting landscape. Students are changing, technology is changing, demands from institutions are changing.

You can't improve in a vacuum. Gather some data to find out what to improve in the first place. You can't read students' minds. Nor can you change everything overnight. Take one step at a time to become the best possible teacher. This project will take many semesters to accomplish.

Here are some questions to ask yourself and issues to consider as you plan for improvement of your class development, teaching, and assessing skills.

Improvement Questions

No Student Left Behind?
Impossible task. If your feelings of success as an instructor are heavily linked to everyone being an academic star in your class, you are doomed to disappointment. *You cannot care more about your students' education than they care themselves.* Your goal is to set up the best possible learning environment, give prompt useful feedback, use formative assessment and make adjustments, teach clearly, grade fairly, motivate as well as you can, and then the rest is student responsibility. You can't run the race for them. But if a large portion of students are failing every semester or a majority are earning "A" grades, you need to examine your expectations, your teaching, and your assessments.

Are students productively involved in cognitively demanding ways?
This is probably the most important question of all. If you punctuate your class with the use of active learning techniques that engage students at the higher levels of Bloom's Taxonomy as well as demand they think carefully and critically, you will be involving students as active participants. Make sure you use the higher levels of Bloom, however, because students hate mindless group busy work, and rightly so. Challenge their minds. Ask essential questions.

Am I boring?

Could be! Videotape yourself and see if you would sleep through your own class. Learn to modulate your voice, use gestures, walk around, be engaging, ask more challenging questions. Fabulous teachers usually do have a bit of theatre in them, or they appear to because they are so enthused about their subject.

Is class boring?

Could be! Use formative assessment and find out! If students feel class is boring, find out what to fix. If you use active learning techniques, this is not going to be a problem.

Do I know the material myself?

Few things are more de-motivating to students than listening to an instructor they don't feel is credible. Read your own textbook! Don't get yourself into situations where you don't really know what you are talking about. Being an expert is NOT the same thing as having answers to everything. Usually it is people who are unsure of their own knowledge who can't say, "I don't know." Experts actually know they can't answer everything that comes up. But you should be highly knowledgeable to teach at college and continually develop professionally. Students can generally pick out a phony, and they are insulted.

Is class challenging enough?

Easy classes are actually de-motivating, especially to fast learners. No one respects them though word gets around and some students still take "easy" classes for the grade.

Too challenging?

Remember, students have to think they have a good chance at success; classes way over their heads aren't likely to get good attendance or effort. For some subjects, the best way to gauge appropriate level of challenge is to pre-test students during the first week. Pre-test them over the material you feel is basic to know entering your class, and the material you might cover in the first month. This will help you set the right challenge level as well as provide extra help to pockets of students who don't quite grasp something essential. It will also help you guide some students right out of your class and into a lower level where they can be successful.

Am I building value connections?

This is an instructor task – show students the value in your subject. It isn't enough that it fascinates you! On the first day you might ask students to write down their majors, interests, and questions they have about the subject, as well as goals for the class. Go over these privately and try hard to build connections to major areas of interest within your lesson designs. Just a one-minute linkage per day will do wonders for motivation, and as you build your connections, students will see ways to build their own. This is a wonderful gift you'll be modeling for them.

Why don't they get this??? Am I confusing?

Could be! Formative assessment will help you find out. Use it. If you do a "What's Confusing?" CAT and ¾ of the class is lost, look at how you structured that lesson. You may need to change things. Are you skipping what you think is too elemental (maybe it is for you, but not for them)? Put in more examples. Break the concept into smaller parts. Build links more deliberately between old and new information. Try a new approach. Remember, don't expect different results if you keep doing the same old thing. Most important, don't blame the students if most of the class is confused.

Is class fun?

No, class doesn't have to be "fun," but humor helps at times. Just be careful that your humor is appropriate. You are in a power position even if you try not to be – teasing humor is generally inappropriate. GAMES are a good, solid source of "fun." You can access a free Jeopardy template, on-line and it works beautifully for review sessions in most subjects. Writing humorous test items is also fun as long as they make sense too. Giving groups humorous scenarios and case studies to work through creates lightness while learning.

Have I built choice into my classes?

This won't work for all classes, but it does work for most. Allow as much choice as possible because students are more motivated to work on problems/issues they choose for themselves. Those are the areas they are most interested in, so it stands to reason. Especially your adult learners want choice. Where can you build in choice?

Do I reward effort?

This is a big issue in some classes, especially math. What if a student does a complicated problem correctly right up until the last decimal point? Is it all wrong? Or do you give partial credit? Obviously the answer *depends*. One solution is to give partial credit for the first half of a semester with the clear understanding that credit for effort/process will stop at midterm. Instructors have to decide on this issue for themselves, but it is worth pondering. How do we take uncertain learners into higher levels of performance if we don't start out with some credit for effort?

What is the class atmosphere?

Do students feel free to ask questions? Of course you might say they *should* feel free, but do they really? Again, this is a formative assessment issue, an indirect measures question. If you ever put a student down rudely for a "stupid" question or an incorrect answer, or allow another student in the class to do this, you will kill the positive class atmosphere so necessary to a true learning environment. Disruptive students who monopolize or are rude to you or others also kill the class atmosphere. Such students need to be dealt with directly and rapidly. You need to stay in charge of creating a good environment. And at the beginning, you should remember you are not yet tenured. I've seen some fairly risky choices of assignments and activities during my years in higher ed. When bringing something like a modern film into class, think through your choices carefully. You may not want to choose a film from the "extreme tip of the edge" (extreme violence, racist, misogynist) because when a student complains about an instructor "setting up a hostile learning environment," it has potentially different consequences for you than the tenured faculty member. Same with language in class. You may love the "F" word, but is it really necessary for the learning environment? Will it free up others to pepper the class with similar language? Once that ball starts rolling it is hard to control.

Is anxiety too high? Am I setting up too much competition?

A high level of anxiety hurts performance and motivation. Under high anxiety conditions, people can't think as clearly. High anxiety can come through high stakes tests (testing only once or twice a semester), putting students on the spot in front of their peers with difficult questions, or a lack of clarity about expectations and procedures (disorganized chemistry labs). Study guides, clarity of expectations, plenty of time to perform, and better questioning techniques can help avoid high anxiety classrooms. Some students despise competition, but I've found that teachers who like competition themselves almost always have a tendency to think competition helps motivate everyone. In general, not so. Competition in class generally diminishes motivation. (Review games are different.)

Do I communicate my own joy in teaching?

Teaching is a fabulous job – it is a privilege to be able to engage other people's minds in learning. Communicate this! But if you don't really feel this way, maybe this isn't the profession for you. Students have antenna out for instructors who would really rather be golfing or doing anything else but teaching. Students are spending their money to be in your class – they want you to want to be there.

Improve with Indirect Measures

I find that "mini" indirect measures on specific projects or teaching techniques give me a wealth of important information and are easy to create. This is one case where Happy Faces work really well. Use two or three questions only. These take 30 seconds tops and give you potentially valuable input. Don't use these after every teaching event, but occasionally you'll want some input about how a technique worked especially the first time you use something different. Examples:

Please assess the video we just saw <u>as a learning activity</u>:

The video clarified some issues and content for me.

The video worksheet was helpful to focus my attention.

Useful as a learning activity, use again next semester.

How could this activity be improved?

Please give me some input on the jigsaw method we just used in class.

The jigsaw seemed to get more people directly involved.

The jigsaw worked well to help me learn the material.

I'd like to use the jigsaw method again this semester.

How could this activity be improved?

Measures of Courses and Strategies

At the institutional level many forms of indirect assessment are probably taking place. The one you are most familiar with is faculty course evaluation. The Research Office generally designs (or purchases), distributes, and crunches the numbers on these indirect measures. Certainly, if you are asked to help make any other institutional survey available to your students during a class-period, you want to cooperate, but beyond that modest contribution, you probably are not too involved.

Many teachers refer to faculty course evaluations as "personality contests" and view results skeptically. It's an old debate, but whether they are or not depends a great deal on their wording. You will generally have enough serious students answering these evaluations to keep the focus on teaching proficiency and away from teacher personality. Before using the forms, ask to look over the questions. All evaluation forms are not created equal. Some are truly awful, actually, or so general that the feedback is of little value. But many colleges let faculty add questions. If that's true where you are teaching, design some questions that serve your specific needs. There may be timelines involved here, so inquire early in the semester about this.

I encourage faculty to design their own, more useful summative indirect course evaluations. I say "more useful" because items on most faculty course evaluations generalize: *"I learned a great deal in this class."* (1 – 5 scoring). What happens if 60% of your class says "NO?" You have no clue what to change. If you design your own course evaluation forms, you can ask questions that give you clearer data. Be sure to keep the forms anonymous and treat them exactly like you do the official college versions: leave the room, have a student collect them and seal them in an envelope in front of the class, and deliver them to the Research Office or Dean. Tell students they will be held until after grades are posted.

A Sample Faculty-Designed Class Evaluation

You want to remind students their effort and attendance had a lot to do with how much they learned. Start your form off with questions that at least make them think about their own efforts. Then ask specific questions you want answered. Questions can be on a broad array of topics from rigor level in the class, fairness of grading, timeliness of feedback, etc. Don't make the forms too long or students will not complete them. Ask only about things you can or are willing to do something about. If you can't change a textbook because the department voted to use it, then there really is no point asking about it. Below are some sample questions and formats. You'll find your own.

Class: English Composition I

My attendance for this class was:

- ☐ Excellent, hardly ever missed
- ☐ Good, missed only two or three
- ☐ Fair, missed four or five classes
- ☐ A bit Poor, missed more than five classes

My effort in this class was:

- ☐ Excellent, I came well prepared and did the readings and assignments
- ☐ Good, I usually came prepared and usually did the homework
- ☐ Fair, I was a little hit and miss with being prepared, skipped some homework
- ☐ A bit Poor, didn't usually read before class, skipped a lot of the homework

As a learning experience....

How did the books work for you?	Amount I Read			Rating of Books			Please explain your Ratings here
				Good	OK	Change	
Olivia	All	Most	Some	Little	O	O	O
Words into Cloth	All	Most	Some	Little	O	O	O
Henderson the Rain King	All	Most	Some	Little	O	O	O
Writing the Paragraph	All	Most	Some	Little	O	O	O

How much did the activities help your learning?	Helped a lot	Was OK	Didn't Learn from this	Please explain your Ratings here
Ted Talk paragraphs	O	O	O	_____ _____ _____
YouTube assignment	O	O	O	_____ _____ _____
Peer Reviews	O	O	O	_____ _____ _____
Critical Thinking Journal	O	O	O	_____ _____ _____
Group Presentation	O	O	O	_____ _____ _____
Small Group Work	O	O	O	_____ _____ _____

Another summative indirect measure to develop is a perception instrument. These are truly "indirect" measures of student outcomes because they have to do with student perceptions of how much they have learned, not their actual performance. Perceptions, of course, are important – if students don't see their own progress the same way you see it (through grading their direct products), then something needs to change.

Here is a nice little way to design these types of measures. Remember, they are perceptions and not a measure of learning. But they help verify patterns you find in student papers, on projects, and on final tests. Interpret with caution. Perceptions are frequently not reality.

Rate your knowledge level on the first day of class.						Rate your knowledge level on the last day of class.				
Low			Fairly High			Low			Fairly High	
1	2	3	4	5	Ability to develop a clear thesis statement	1	2	3	4	5
1	2	3	4	5	Ability to proofread my own work and catch errors	1	2	3	4	5

I think there is value in having students sign their names to perception instruments. There is a certain amount of accountability involved, and you can compare what they reported to how you have charted their growth over the semester. Having students fill out a copy of the left side of this instrument during the first week of class is also useful for you. It is then serving in a somewhat diagnostic capacity. If three-quarters of your class reports they have high skills with something, well, this is pretty easy to check out. Have them perform! If they were accurate, perhaps you do not need to cover that topic for the full week planned or you can set up groups with peer-to-peer tutoring potential. All win-win. Used at the end of the semester, you will still want to treat these instruments like the official anonymous surveys; have a student collect them and take them to the Research Office for safe keeping until grades are posted.

The Visit from Your Supervisor

Expect your supervisor to observe your teaching at least once a term when you are new at a college. This is one way colleges try to help new faculty improve. These observations are usually scheduled in advance, but some supervisors forget to observe their instructors. Many deans are extremely busy (or disorganized). But if your supervisor forgets, this is not necessarily a good thing. If you are a good instructor, you want to be observed and have this recorded! If your supervisor does not observe your teaching in person, any future references from them will have to be based only on student evaluations. *Invite* your supervisor to come observe you.

Plan ahead for the observation. Ask if you can see what form (if any) your supervisor will be using. Make certain everything will run smoothly and don't spend half the class period testing. Show your stuff!! Then follow up in a week or two and ask for feedback. You may get some tips from your dean that actually help you – or not. Either way, ask your dean some specific questions showing you are eager to improve: *"Do you have some techniques for getting more students involved in discussions? I'd really like to perfect that. Sometimes it works well, but I'd like it to be more consistent. Do you have any suggestions?"*

Checklist: Assessment, Grading, and Continual Improvement

❑ Check for a college-wide grading scale you have to use. Or is there an unofficial grading scale to consider?

❑ Think deeply about the nature of your subject area and how important it is to this student and the people depending upon this student's skills in the future. Develop your grading scale accordingly. For example, in a course for medical lab technicians on typing blood, should a student be able to pass if accurate only 70% of the time? 80%? 90%? At 90% accuracy, a student is likely to kill one in 10 patients by mislabeling blood. Some classes must work at the mastery level: students must master the material to pass.

❑ Structure your point system so students can't get an "A" if they do not have an "A" knowledge level.

❑ Develop a system to communicate grades while still protecting privacy.

❑ Develop a policy for making up quizzes, classes, tests, and assignments that can be fair to all students and allow some "life events" to happen without destroying their grade.

❑ Plan for as many objectively graded assessments as possible.

❑ Place all important grading issues in the syllabus.

❑ Keep grades in more than one place.

❑ Develop good grading rubrics ahead of time and give them to students as guides way before projects are due.

❑ Realize rubrics will always be in need of slight improvements. Make the improvements.

❑ Establish ways to effectively grade discussion and any group work.

❑ Use "in – progress" evaluation forms for any group projects, several times during the semester.

❑ Decide which major concepts to use formative direct assessment on. Create/choose the best one for the concept.

- ❏ Use comprehensive summative tests and projects for the end of the course. Cover several major objectives.
- ❏ Modify your textbook's test bank to fit your own objectives and audience.
- ❏ Have a trusted colleague review any test items you develop yourself while you are still learning.
- ❏ Use a variety of testing formats, but choose deliberately so you match up purpose and test item type.
- ❏ Use test item analysis to examine your items for quality, miskeys, challenge level, etc. Easy if your tests are on-line.
- ❏ Locate your department's assessment plan and check to make sure you're following it, if required.
- ❏ Locate faculty course evaluation forms and review them. Ask if you can add your own questions.
- ❏ Design your own course evaluations. Make sure you can do this. There may be a process or approval to go through.
- ❏ Design indirect measures for activities. Use student suggestions for improvement.
- ❏ Prepare for your supervisor's observations. Ask for feedback. Ask for an observation if they seem to have skipped you.

Skill 11:

USE ON-LINE ELEMENTS EFFECTIVELY

There are many good resources on best practices for teaching on-line classes. Numerous research studies as well as entire industries are focused on this topic. Perhaps your college is even already a member of Quality Matters, an organization that specializes in on-line class development, staff training, etc. If you get assigned an on-line class, be sure to check. It is beyond the intent of this book to tell you how to set up and run a complete on-line class when all you have to do is google *"Best Practice in Online Education"* to be immersed in information, much of it directly from the Big Ten research universities with evidence to back it up.

Having taught on-line for many years, my goal here is to give you some quick tips and practical advice on using on-line elements effectively, even if you do not teach a whole class on-line. Students generally expect you to use on-line components.

What you will have, more than likely, is a face-to-face class where students want a few class elements easily accessible on-line. You will need to learn a few things about your school's eLearning Management System. There are many different types of systems, but they are all fairly similar in what they can do for you. Get the help you need before the semester starts. If there is a mini seminar for new teachers on using the system, go. More senior instructors can help, and of course the IT department almost always has dedicated staff to assist faculty. Don't get frustrated if on-line isn't your interest or your strength. The IT folks and the CTL director (at your campus Center for Teaching and Learning) can help you with anything like adding a test item.

Little Bits of On-Line for Face-to-Face Classes

There are effective ways to use just a "little bit" of on-line to your advantage in any face-to-face class.

- Always put your syllabus on-line
- Develop a little test item over your syllabus that says simply "I have read and understood the syllabus" – where students have to "agree" in order to move forward into the class.

OR

- Put a much more extensive set of test items up about the syllabus and about the class requirements in general. Students will have the same "Agree" to move forward with each item. Basically, this is obtaining their 'signature'. It will help them clearly understand what the class is all about.

Sample items:

"I understand there are three major papers in this class, one due each four weeks."

"I understand the 3 papers make up 45% of the grade in this class."

"I understand that there is a final comprehensive exam in this course, which is worth 20% of my grade."

"I understand that my consistent attendance is required and that after 4 class misses I receive an automatic grade penalty of…."

"I understand that if I cannot make class for a serious reason I should…."

"I understand it is my responsibility to come prepared with the readings and homework done for each class."

"I understand it is my responsibility to be an active participant in discussion and application exercises."

"I understand that my participation in discussions will be graded and count for 15% of my grade in this class."

"I understand that each graded element in this class is 'weighted' (worth a % of my grade)."

- Put your grading rubrics on-line way before the papers or projects they assess are due. Students always have access to them then.
- You may want to use the Dropbox function (the name may differ between LMS but this is the place where students can drop their papers electronically). You can grade the papers on-line then and also leave your feedback there.
- Learn to use the Gradebook function. You can keep students up on their grades much easier.
- Using Gradebook has another advantage. You can use a weighted system for grades which allows much more flexibility in number of points you give to each assignment. When using a weighted system, the points are not necessarily what is added up over the semester for a grade. It is the % each assignment is worth that counts. Thus, if a paper is worth 10 points or 70 points, it doesn't really matter – because what matters is that the paper is worth 10% of the course grade. Sounds complicated but isn't. I have found this to be the

most adaptable system over time. For instance, if "Activities in Class" were 20% of the grade and snow days canceled three class periods, this is not a problem with the weighted system. The remaining days still will calculate up as 20%. If you had used a point system you have to go in and make adjustments because now all your point totals are off. Besides – it's fun to have a machine do all the math for you. The LMS Gradebook makes using a weighted system very easy. All you have to do is decide what percentage of the total grade each major element is worth: Papers, 20%, Project, 10%, Speech, 10%, Activities, 20%, Homework, 20%, Tests, 20%. You get the idea.

- Use on-line discussion questions to get students reading for class. Open some discussion questions students must answer before class for credit. You can open and close these so the next set opens up automatically right after class for the next class, then closes access right when class starts.

- Put up homework apply sheets or other types of challenging problems students must print off, fill out, and bring to class with them. Again, this helps students come prepared if the sheets are worth points.

- Learn to make little video files and put them up for students. You can be a talking head or you can focus on your hands showing a math problem, a process, drawing a mind map, installing a part, pointing out differences between two easily confused plant species, reviewing the settings on a CNC machine – all from the comfort of your office or lab. If you don't want to make video, the audio is particularly easy and also useful. Audio: think about explaining a particularly difficult concept with additional examples building on the ones you used in class. All you need is your laptop. Video: think about a bear of a proof that usually confuses students but now they can watch your hand and mind in action over and over until they understand. This use of video and audio on-line to present information is really a major element of the flipped classroom but you can be just a "little bit flipped" and use it occasionally. It's a way of reinforcing learning without your having to explain the same item over and over. Let the computer do it for you. It's kind of fun, too, and students really like it.

Best Practices Overview

If you teach on-line or have a "hybrid" class where part of it is on-line, remember these practices recommended by many experts:

❑   First, it is critical to be organized! Your on-line class should be easy to navigate. When students can't find something like Content they become very frustrated. What seems organized to you may be confusing to students using the on-line system for the first time. If you have some colleagues or friends who will run through the class and tell you if it felt easy to navigate and seemed logically structured, great. It's nice to find someone to do this who isn't familiar with the LMS system because many of your students aren't either.

❑ Decide which elements (Discussion? Groups? Live chat? Etc.) are right to use for your particular class. Elements need to have a learning purpose. Most platforms have more elements than you'll want to use. Discussion is one element that is sometimes overused. Will it really help students master the objectives?

❑ Provide Checklists or something similar, which walk students through the class step-by-step, especially when you are using several different types of assignments.

❑ Communicate due dates in more than one place. In the dawn of the on-line class, some instructors had no due dates; they just had a self-paced class that students moved through at their own speed. As long as all the assignments were done by the end of the semester, students were in the clear. I see two major flaws in this system: 1, students ended up failing or taking IPs (In Progress) or Incompletes frequently because they procrastinated until a week before the end of the semester; 2, instructors were simply overwhelmed with grading a gazillion assignments before the semester close and probably didn't do such a good job of it either. Have due dates. Communicate them several places.

❑ A semester schedule works just as well for on-line as face-to-face classes. Yes, there is probably a Calendar element in your LMS, but a Schedule that is printable and shows the entire semester at a glance is very helpful to some students. Surprisingly, not all on-line students are familiar with technology, and they will appreciate being able to print that schedule!

❑ All the instructor qualities you demonstrate in a face-to-face class (respect, friendliness, professionalism, humanness, caring) somehow need to be conveyed in an on-line class too. It's just harder. But consider making a few little videos that you scatter throughout the class so students get to know you. It could be a one-minute talk about how exciting the next topic is to you, or talk about how pleased you were with the discussion posts and give the reasons why. You want to make sure students know you care about them and that you are not a robot.

❑ Use some type of ice-breaker so students can start recognizing each others' names and build an on-line community.

❑ Encourage a lot of faculty/student interaction. This can be through comments, chats, phone calls, virtual office hours, personal emails, etc.

❏ Provide fast turnaround on graded assignments. Prompt feedback is essential in any class, but perhaps even more so in the on-line class, which happens in more of a vacuum. Students need feedback.

❏ Leave comments on-line for graded projects and check to see students have read them. You may even require students to respond so there is some interaction going. A really nice touch is to make a 30-second personal video with your feedback and encouragement, emailed directly to the student. These don't really take much more time than typing up the same information. There are free web aps that allow you to easily make these; all you need is a laptop. Ask your CTL leader or the office responsible for on-line tech help for advice. They usually have more ideas than anyone uses!

❏ You still need to use active learning and critical thinking activities on-line. You can even create groups and have them submit a single project. The activities make class far more learning centered than the old "read the chapters and take the tests and write one paper" style of on-line classes. You want students interacting with other students, working as a team, commenting on discussions, doing peer reviews, etc.

❏ Ask for what you want and stick to it. Years ago, I wanted students to answer discussion questions with more than an opinion, so the discussion rubric clearly said a reliable resource had to be used (beyond the textbook) and had to be linked or cited within each Post just to get graded. Invariably during the first discussion, several good students would write about 500 words of excellent Post but not include a resource. Someone else would write 80 words and include a resource. The first couple semesters I went ahead and gave points to good work even if it didn't have a resource; I felt bad about not grading good work. I emailed everyone and said to reread the rubric and include a resource next time. Well, only about half did. I had to email again. And again. I was complaining to a colleague who simply said: *"Good grief, follow your own rubric and you'll get what you want."* So true. The next semester all students who posted their first discussion without a reference received a zero. That really got their attention! Panic among a few. But because I had 12 discussions during the semester and dropped the lowest 2 scores in the end, their oversight didn't hurt grades. Always remember students come to you fairly unskilled. When you can find ways to ask for what you want and stick to it without hurting their chance of success, then you are positively shaping their behaviors.

❏ Learn to be a great teacher in your face-to-face classes and translate what works there into the on-line environment. What students need and want doesn't change just because they are on-line.

Skill 12:

AVOID THE BIG MISTAKES
Safety, Ethics, and Legalities

The job of teaching is more than content delivery and grading. While your class is in session, you are THE responsible person in the room or lab or on the field trip. Having spent almost the last three decades somewhere in higher ed, I have seen some mistakes made, sometimes with serious penalties. I'd like to help you avoid them all. But you will have to take it upon yourself to find out some of the key information here because very few colleges will actually be directly addressing most of these points with their new faculty. Yes, they will tell you to read the faculty handbook. And you should. The points below require thinking ahead.

Safety

- What are the sexual assault stats for your campus? Do you teach a night class where you or your students have to walk back to dorms or dark parking lots? Set up a Buddy System or get numbers for the campus escort service. All large campuses have these to assure their students make it back to their dorms and cars safely. Make your students aware of this, especially your female students. It can be pretty scary as a 19-year-old female to walk alone at 10 p.m. through a maze of dark hallways and between buildings to reach a destination. If any student is uneasy, call security to escort them. Small campuses may not have any escort services or security so the Buddy System is essential.

- Do you know the campus security number? Do you know who to call if a student is threatening another student or threatening you? It doesn't have to be overt, either, to be seriously upsetting. Do you carry your cell phone with you so you could call? I had a young teaching colleague who was having consistent trouble with an outspoken, broody male student in a night class. One night she dismissed her class and took some time getting her papers all stacked up, technology turned off, etc. Then she looked up and found this student walking by her classroom. Then again. Then back he came again. A chill ran through her. This is the feeling to pay attention to – your animal insides know when there is a threat. We have a tendency to talk ourselves out of those feelings because we don't want to appear silly, biased, or weak. But she walked over to the door and locked it and called campus security. When they came down the hall the student walked off. Oh, they met with the Dean of Students later and settled a few things, too.

- Do you teach in a blizzard? Who makes the decision to cancel class for weather? Even on the residential mega campuses, a percentage of students drive to college sometimes from long distances. Are teachers allowed to cancel individual classes for weather? I never wanted to be the one who said, *"You have to come to class regardless; put your life in danger on ice-packed roads to get here for a lecture on Freud."* Really? So think this one through. If the campus is closed, you have no decision. If the campus doesn't close but you have students driving 30 miles and the weather is horrible, do you penalize them for not coming? Do you know how many long distance commuters you have? You'll need to find out some campus specific information and then put a policy in your syllabus.
- Tornadoes. Do you know where to take your class if the alarm goes off?
- Drunk or otherwise drugged students in class? Students who suffer from mental illness and have a meltdown? Do you know who to call for help? Do you have a phone?
- Shooters. Unfortunately, this does rarely, rarely happen, but surely most campuses do have a system for handling it by now. Find out what you are supposed to do. My husband teaches at a Community College, and they went on lock-down for a shooting in the immediate neighborhood once. They had a set of rules to follow right in the classroom: first, lock the door, second, align the students on the side of the room where they couldn't be seen through the door window, third, don't leave until an official all clear is heard through the sound system. They waited 45 minutes for that all clear to sound. It was pretty spooky. But they followed directions. Can you find these directions for your own campus?

Ethics

You are in a power position. That requires a certain level of thoughtfulness about how you interact with students. It seems these things shouldn't even need to be said, but they do. I've seen faculty in their 40s get non-renewed for too many rumors/reports about questionable ethics with students. And don't think these suggestions are all to protect students. Some students may become attracted to you – but you can't go there with them. There are certainly students with large ambitions, larger egos, and some mental imbalance who can set faculty up for disaster. Again, rare, but still – just think ahead.

- ALWAYS keep your office door open when meeting with a student of either gender. ALWAYS.
- You are a compassionate teacher. You are not a Buddy. You are not a Counselor (unless you are). If a student needs a counselor, you should have that number ready to give them, but you should not be reaching out to help students with mental health issues or life crises yourself. You do not meet students at the local burger place for a beer to discuss their girlfriend issues, even if they want you to. Your campus has expert help for students in need.
- No, you don't date students. Not while they are in your class.
- You don't kid around with sexually charged humor with students. It can easily get out of hand or misinterpreted.
- You don't go out just to drink with a few students.
- Do not share private information students blurted out while you were looking for the Counseling Office number – with anyone.
- Don't hug. Hugs mean different levels of affection for different people and in different cultures. They are easily misinterpreted. Some people are compulsive huggers when they think someone "needs a hug" or they are excited to see someone. If you are one of these hugging types, restrain yourself. Hugging and putting your arm around someone can come back to haunt you. Think about the arm you placed warmly around someone's shoulders as you walk down the hall. Would you do that to your supervisor? No. Why not? Besides their personality, you can't see yourself putting your arm around a higher ranked individual with more power than you have. Students feel the same way. Most will not be comforted by your warm friendly arm, they will feel more powerless by its weight. I had a president at one college who loved to walk women down the hall with his arm draped in a friendly manner around their shoulders, chatting away. Some were Deans, some were staff. It didn't take more than 3 – 4 months on the job and multiple unhappy people had reported him to HR. Now that was a very uncomfortable talk for the Human Resources Director, I'm sure! The president was floored, extremely unhappy, embarrassed and angry; he was a friendly soul who was just trying to be accepted in his new position. But he didn't think ahead about the power of that position.

There are other ethical issues too, of course, beyond relationship ones:

- Show up for class yourself! Students paid for your class. Show up early. Leave late. Be available for your class, completely, during the whole timeslot. When you teach a lab section, be there the whole time, don't wander off and leave students to themselves. Don't cancel class to take your children trick-or-treating.

- Follow through. If you say you'll do something like bring in the answer to someone's question next class period, then do it. This will make you a little more careful about what you promise.
- Remember you are there to help students learn content and critical thinking, you are not in class to spread your political or religious views, ever.
- Treat everyone equally…or fairly? This isn't a trick question. I was teaching English Composition for an IU campus one year and had a difficult situation. The first essay came in, and a young woman from Korea wrote a paper comparing the economic systems of Brazil and France. It was an amazingly fascinating paper, but it was riddled with grammar errors. English was this young woman's third or fourth language, and she wasn't fluent yet. In the same class another young woman turned in a paper on how to prepare for a first date. It was tepid and shallow, but the English was pretty flawless. All adjuncts were supposed to use the same rubric to grade essays, which had a strict allowance for errors in spelling, grammar, syntax, etc. Five errors and the paper was an automatic F. So, what would you do? What would be the *ethical* thing to do?
- Do you know who is in your chain of command? You probably have a supervisor (Dean? Department Chair?), but suppose you can't relate to them, honestly don't trust them, or find they are no help at all? Who do you go to next for help with really challenging situations? You would do well to find a faculty mentor with years of experience because you will definitely run into ethical dilemmas. If you aren't sure about how to move forward in a situation, you want to talk to someone you trust.
- Does your college have an ombudsperson? Find out. They can help you work through difficult situations. The University of Iowa's Office of the Ombudsperson has an excellent explanation of their role: "The Office of the Ombudsperson is a resource for any member of the university community – including students, faculty, and staff –with a problem or concern. We provide informal conflict resolution, mediation services and advocacy for fair treatment and fair process. Services are confidential."

Legalities

Certainly there are legalities that go beyond this list, but if you are teaching the content without blunt bias and grading fairly and are evenhanded and professional in dealings with your students, you'll have no problems at all. But here are a few minor thoughts:

- How long are you legally supposed to hang on to student papers?
- What is the policy for keeping attendance records? Or taking attendance so you are in compliance with federal financial aid regulations?
- How long do you keep a gradebook?
- What is the campus policy on plagiarism? Other types of cheating? Can you make up your own rules in this area?
- What really is Academic Freedom? What does it mean to you, the new instructor?
- What information can you share with your students' parents? (none without a signed student release, but how do you know they signed one?)
- Can a spouse or roommate pick up another student's paper? (no)
- Who can even answer these types of questions if they aren't in the handbook of policies? Is it HR? (You need the handbook.)
- Does your college have a lawyer on retainer? Who can access this individual if they do? With what questions?
- What kicks in mandatory reporting at your college?
- Keep documentation about conversations with difficult students or a difficult dean, etc., including emails. Don't hit "delete" too fast.
- Never say anything in email you don't want in the newspaper.

Skill 13:

AVOID ANNOYING YOUR STUDENTS/
BECOME EFFECTIVE

The Behavior of Annoying Teachers

- Read the syllabus on Day One word-for-word, all class – boring!
- Tell students how many will fail the class on day One
- Say anything is boring, as in *"This chapter is really boring, but we have to cover it…"*
- Waste time
  - Too much time taking roll each day; Too much time passing out papers
  - Too much time getting the activities organized; Too much time fumbling with technology
- Talk about personal life when it's a tangent
- Make class too easy or blazingly difficult
- Ignore instead of handle rude or disruptive students
- Let some students completely dominate discussions
- Tolerate slackers always coming in late; tolerate sleepers
- Lean toward Disorganization – take up class time to put themselves in order
- Lack the ability to explain difficult concepts clearly and carefully
- Defensive; not really answering questions
- Never ask students what they think
- Come to class late regularly; Leave class early regularly; cancel classes
- Offer nothing new – go straight from the textbook
- Require books but never use them or only a little part of them
- Put materials on reserve in the library and have too few for the size of class
- Add assignments mid-semester that weren't on the syllabus
- Make students feel stupid by being snide; using anything but a professional tone of voice
- Berate the entire class for something like overall poor performance (good students get mad)
- Act like they'd rather be doing anything else besides teaching
- Talk about how poorly they are paid; Complain about the administration, their office quarters, etc.

- Give hours of PowerPoint lecture; drone on and on with little application or interaction; No breaks in long classes
- Don't seem like a real expert in their field
- Have trick test items; poorly constructed and confusing test items; only a few big tests for the semester
- Give away good grades to people who do not earn them
- Monotone voice; not speaking loud enough; not writing clearly
- Use stupid, babyish activities; busy work
- Don't monitor Group projects – slackers get a good grade because others worked hard
- Use inappropriate humor while thinking they are funny
- Clearly play favorites – whether it's to the women, the men, the football stars, or any group
- Give poor feedback; not timely; "good job" instead of real feedback
- Aren't clear about how projects or papers will be graded
- Keep class over time as if students didn't have another class to get to across campus

Effective Teachers

Considerable research has gone into finding out what makes an effective teacher. It's good to look over this list at the beginning of a semester and again at the end to see how you would grade yourself against these practices. Teaching is always a work in progress, however, so don't get discouraged. Add something new each semester and you'll end up with an admirable skill set.

Effective Teachers
- ❏ Know their subject matter thoroughly
- ❏ Plan their course goals, objectives, and activities, are clear and organized
- ❏ Involve students actively in learning
- ❏ Display warmth and enthusiasm
- ❏ Engage students' minds in critical thinking
- ❏ Plan their questioning in advance
- ❏ Let students know they love teaching and their subject area
- ❏ Continually strive to gather information from students
- ❏ Use student feedback to improve their skills as teachers
- ❏ Teach holistically – embed skills/knowledge/attitudes and behaviors to be learned within real applications – remembering the whole person

Skill 14:

START WISELY: SIDESTEP THE ELEPHANTS IN ACADEMIA

Avoiding the Elephants

Academic environments have those unmentionable elephants hiding in plain sight just like most big organizations. What? Elephants in the halls here too? You bet. You have entered a political landscape. So I will point out a few areas you'll want to be cautious about or simply ignore. It is best for you to start on the right foot by keeping it out of your mouth and firmly on the floor (at least until you are tenured and perhaps forever after).

Your colleagues

- You'll hear things from students: this teacher is easy, this teacher is hard, this teacher grades unfairly, this teacher cancels class all the time, this teacher is mean to us, this teacher just lectures and we're bored, we're not learning anything, etc. What do you do? Do not get involved with discussing hearsay about other teachers. There is a pretty standard response: *"Did you discuss this with the teacher?"* When students say "no" or "I'm not comfortable" its on to "I can't really discuss other teachers, but there are people you can talk to at the college – here are their names and numbers." The exception here is abuse. In that case you need to march the student to college reporting authorities yourself.

- You can't change your colleagues' personalities and habits. Accept that up front and you'll be happier. Control what you can: yourself and how you run your class.
- Colleagues can help or hinder you. Colleagues who genuinely like you are more likely to support you in general, which is especially good during tenure and budget processes. A pain-in-the-ass untenured faculty member is way too easy to get rid of. Don't be one. Make friends. Please rise above the forest of egos if you find yourself surrounded by them and avoid the cynics. Besides, at the beginning, you don't know who has built alliances with whom, who used to date whom, etc. Stay maturely on the sidelines of gossip and do not discuss teachers with other teachers in any negative manner.

Help for You
- Don't expect much help getting up and running as a quality teacher. Orientations are usually about policy, not teaching or assessing. If your college is different, wonderful!! But accept the fact you usually have to teach yourself by finding resources like this book. Reading and applying it will definitely help. Find your CTL (Center for Teaching and Learning) or its equivalent.
- Mentors assigned by colleges are sometimes not the best. They may be eager volunteers perhaps but not necessarily great teachers. Ask around and find out who is really a great teacher in many peoples' eyes. See if they will let you watch them teach and maybe mentor you.

Deans
- Don't like your dean? Wait another year – they will likely be gone. Deans spin through jobs (and may land at a college where you will apply next). Don't participate in a favorite college sport: "dean bashing." They have it rough. True, some lack competence, communication skill, or integrity. They are humans, after all, and they are 'at will' employees. Deans are the filling in an Oreo cookie: admin presses down from the top with demands, and faculty press up from the bottom, and deans get thinner and thinner. It is best to assume they have good intent, and you don't have the full story anyway.
- Deans do not like surprises, especially when the problems will run uphill. Always keep deans informed of dicey issues like a large-scale cheating situation, but also share the good: student wins a competition. Just don't overwhelm them with day-to-day trivia and questions even if they said "stop by any time." (They didn't really expect you to.)

Committee Work

- Don't get sucked into too much committee work! You will attract invitations to join committees like barns attract flies. If you aren't careful you will be over-committed and feeling crazed. Your first 2 to 3 years should be all about becoming a polished instructor, not a committee maven. Best excuse ever: *I am a new instructor, and I just want to focus on being the best teacher I can be for my students right now. Be sure to ask me again in a couple years.*

- Avoid political or complex committees, but choose one to join. You have to serve the college contractually, so ask a few seasoned faculty which committees to avoid. Some are fraught with political tension and put you into conflict situations no new teacher needs. The Safety Committee is generally considered safe territory! Diversity? Curriculum? Assessment? Perhaps not at the start.

Conflict with Students

- Avoid it. Deans do not like to sit with crying or swearing students in their office talking about what you said to them. Conflict takes two to escalate. Always be the professional. Keep a calm tone of voice. Document frequently if you have a difficult student in class. The key is documentation and clear expectations written down and signed off on by students the first week.

- Don't assume the Dean will side with you. Sometimes they do, sometimes they don't. If you don't have clear policies, assignments, due dates, written down and distributed to all students and consistently enforced, you may not be supported if a student protests a requirement change or a grade. With clear expectations/policies/etc. and signed slips saying students read and understood them, the worst Dean almost always has to stand by a faculty member. Plan ahead.

Hand Holding, Rigor, and Retention Shenanigans

- There are students in your classes who should not be there. They are not ready for college, not really interested in college, and are so ill prepared almost everything you teach is a mile beyond them. Unless your college is massively unique, you will be encouraged to hold their hands and do almost anything in your power to retain, retain, retain students. You may have a coach or dean call you up and ask if there is "anything we can do about Johnny." If Johnny has 26% as his accumulated final grade in your class and you have the documentation to prove it – good for you. You should. You should also tell the caller you would be happy to sit with them and the VP of Academics and go over Johnny's accumulation of points together. (They will decline this polite invitation.) Report any such pressure call to your Dean (unless it was him/her; if so, go higher).

- Do take part in the early warning systems most colleges have to alert advisors that students aren't coming to class, are failing, etc. What degree of additional shepherding you decide to do is up to each teacher. Some call a student if they miss class. Some don't. Some send email reminders of due dates. Some feel strongly this is not shaping professional behaviors and attitudes needed in any career. Decide for yourself.

- Rigor needs to remain high. Do you really want a paramedic who passed with D grades? A civil engineer who scraped through classes on their sparkling personality? No. They can hurt people. You will find discussions of rigor are primarily academic in nature (everyone agrees we need it) – but the huge push to retain rules back in the classrooms of many teachers. Be true to the level of danger inherent in the jobs your students will take. Would you send a poorly qualified lineman out to repair 7000–volt lines? I hope not. You will get a great deal of pressure about retention. Think about the consequences of retaining and passing poorly performing students long and hard before you start getting easier and easier. No matter how good you get at teaching, you will simply not be able to get everyone to learn. But there is more than one reason to get super good at teaching. Look below.

Job Security
- Student enrollment usually drives your job security. (Oh no!) HR doesn't mention this when they hire you, but don't assume once you land a college job you are set for life. Programs close. History and English and math and agriculture departments suffer budget cutbacks and lay off the last hired no matter how brilliant their teaching. Departments are merged and faculty let go. Bad tenured faculty can be fired. It takes a bit of work on the part of administrators, but it can be done even in a highly unionized college.

- Your best job security lies in becoming an outstanding teacher. Good students will keep your classes full by word of mouth. Better yet, with teaching expertise, you maximize the chances those marginal students will perk up and surprise us all, learning and retaining.

Balance Your Time. Don't Burn Out

How do you avoid burnout as you start in this demanding job? It's an issue when you have several different classes to teach, you may have never taught, and you feel like you are only staying about two days ahead of the students. On top of this, you are asked to be on committees. Attend meetings. Make curriculum decisions. Submit assessment plans. Perhaps even help plan for program reviews. And meanwhile, too many students seem bored and unmotivated. Who knew that college students would skip class so much even when you tell them it is important to attend? It's a pretty darned complex job situation, and from the outside it looks so *easy*.

The key is consciously developing balance. You can't devote 20 hours of every 24-hour day to the college. Accepting that you cannot do it all the first year or two will help you stay balanced.

Learn to say NO. Remember the refrain? *"No, that sounds like a worthy project, but I'm still learning to be the best teacher I can be, so maybe next year?"*

Learn to do a little every day (grading, feedback, etc.) so you aren't procrastinating. These chores build up into mountains. Twenty minutes a day grading saves a whole lot of trouble later.

Learn to use practical resources. This little book has dozens of tips for keeping students engaged, learning, and paying attention. Use them. Start with only three tips. Don't try to change everything at once. You'll find when your class is engaged with active learning techniques, teaching isn't nearly as exhausting. You'll feel energized after a good teaching day instead of ready for a beer and nap.

Understand you are probably not going to be an A+ teacher at the start. No one is. The goal is to keep improving your skills over the entire course of your career. No one knows it all in this field. No one does it all. Cut yourself some slack, but be sure you are attempting to continually develop your expertise as a teacher.

Learn how to streamline your evaluation processes through using rubrics, checklists, and other types of grading tools. Rubrics save time for you and provide a more reliable grading process too.

It's easy to get all your mental energy and time sucked into this job. But you may have a spouse or partner, children, aging parents, horses or pets who also need your time. Life is rarely a balance between just two roles; we all play many roles on this stage. Know what is really, really important and carve out time for it (or them) frequently. Many teachers are so pleased to get their job in the first place they don't think hard enough about the human costs of devoting themselves first to the college. But you get the idea. Make the right time sacred, whether it is exercise time running, training your dog, or time with a small child. Don't rob time set aside for yourself and your family to do something for the college that really does not have to be done. Nothing is more stressful than emotional turmoil with people you love, so avoid it! A relaxed mind and body will serve you better in all your roles.

Figure out priorities and allot an appropriate amount of time to each of them. This requires the ability to think ahead and organize before any crisis arises. It helps if you set yourself up fully for a calm semester before you start to teach.

Be Professional

Teachers don't wear tank tops, do they? What does "professional" really mean in the field of college teaching? Well, it means a lot more than dress standards (which are quite relaxed in academia). There are codes of conduct members of any profession share. There will be written rules for faculty (find the handbook somewhere) and unwritten rules having to do with ethics and morals, and yes, how to dress. Teachers don't wear tank tops while teaching if you want to be taken seriously by two groups: your students and your colleagues/supervisors. When you appear to take your profession seriously your students will cut you a little slack. If you appear too similar to the 18 year olds sitting in front of you, the road to engaging and grading them gets harder.

Teachers are generally social animals. We prefer people enjoy us, but this is not supposed to be the outcome for your class – the outcome is student learning. Some teachers have trouble with this one. They so want their students to like them and think they are "cool" (or whatever the current equivalent of *cool* is) that they cross lines attempting to win their students' admiration.

Your role is not "awesome cool buddy," so avoid attempts to put yourself across that way. It is hard to fairly grade "friends." And, if you cast yourself in the role of "buddy," students will have confused expectations for their own behaviors. Maintain a professional, respectful, friendly presence. That doesn't mean you can't also be silly at times and throw out candy to groups with the best answers to questions, but it does mean establishing and maintaining professional boundaries. Should you go out drinking with your current class of students? Not wise. You can still share personal stories which are appropriate to the subject at hand or tell students you are having a "bad day." Students want you to be a fully human being, but students also have expectations for college instructors. When you fit their own mental schema of professional college instructor, they know what to expect and are actually more comfortable.

You are a model for how someone in your field conducts themselves. If you need your students to act like professionals when they graduate as accountants, for example, then you are one of their primary models. You will be showing them how professionals continually solve problems and use self-learning in your field as well as demonstrating the technical language of the area over and over. How you conduct yourself is part of the powerful 'hidden' curriculum influencing all students.

Communicate

With Students
- Return phone calls and emails promptly. Be available before and after class.
- Keep records of any correspondence so you have a "trail." Make a note after any meeting with an unhappy student with time, date, and highlights of conversation.
- Give weekly feedback to each student if at all possible.
- Keep your stated office hours. It is very frustrating for students to try to catch an instructor during their posted office hours only to find the office locked (you didn't come in) or empty (you're at the copy machine).

With Administration
- Keep in email contact with your faculty contact and/or with your supervisor. Tell them the positives that are happening…get help with problems.
- Keep a paper or email trail of correspondence so he-said/she-said is minimized on important issues.
- Warn administration if there is a serious issue. They hate being in the dark or blindsided.
- A very good tip: after a meeting with administration, write back the parties involved, thanking them for the meeting and reiterating point-by-point your understanding of what was discussed. Invite them to clarify if they had a different recollection. Memories can be fuzzy for anyone. But this way you have a tacit agreement on what was said/discussed.
- Ask administration for help when you need the Big Guns, like support with a cheating issue you are uncomfortable handling alone.

With Colleagues

- Don't be in a big rush to get in and out each day. Make friends with other faculty. Chat with them, ask them questions, get to know them personally. They are your best allies and best problem-solvers.
- Be sure to communicate all the good times you experience, too. Build collegial friendships of positive thinking people.
- Help your colleagues with projects: assessment plans, surveys, research, etc.
- Attend all meetings in your department that you can – participate. This screams out "I'm a Team Player."
- *More* communication is better than less communication.

Final Words

I truly wish you the best in your teaching semesters to come! No matter how our students engage with our material, it is still a privilege to be a college teacher. It is also a deep responsibility. It's a little frightening sometimes to look out over our classes and realize these are the very people who will be designing and building the hotels we walk into, saving friend's lives, doing our taxes, inventing software we use, teaching our grandchildren, caring for our aging parents, our forests, our cars, our farmland, as well as voicing and voting on issues dear to our hearts for decades to come.

Get to know your students. When you are old, they will be running the world. Some days that is a terrifying thought. But time passes, and, yes, they will indeed be the ones in charge in fewer years than anticipated. Help them learn respect by respecting them. Help them internalize critical thinking skills so they can make better decisions for themselves and our planet throughout their lives. Our society will depend upon their education and wisdom. Teach your students to ponder issues carefully, ask essential questions, and understand the difference between evidence-based facts and personal opinions. Help them believe in the power of science and data and human kindness. Help them recognize they must continually make the effort to improve their thinking and their compassion. All together, this will make them an educated and wise person.

When you choose this profession, you become a continual student yourself. If one approaches teaching correctly, it makes you humble. It isn't very easy to master. But helping others learn is truly an honor. Chant that to yourself on the lean days; celebrate it on the good days. There will be ample good days. Enjoy.

ABOUT THE AUTHOR

Dr. Patricia Linehan has been involved in higher education for almost three decades. She started out, as so many faculty do, as an adjunct with a Masters degree at a Big Ten university. That got her hooked on teaching. Patricia went on to finish a Ph.D. in Educational Psychology at Purdue University, and entered fulltime into a career in education. Over the years she has taught adjunct or fulltime for Indiana University-Kokomo, St. Mary's (MN), Minnesota State University-Mankato, William Penn University, South Central Community and Technical College, and Southwest Minnesota State University. Patricia served as the Director of Assessment for William Penn in Iowa and the Dean of Research, Planning and Development for South Central in Minnesota. She has given dozens of workshops on assessment techniques, communication, critical thinking, and active teaching to community and technical college faculty and staff. Currently, Dr. Linehan works for Southwest Minnesota State University in a specialized program teaching new community and technical college colleagues to become exceptional faculty. When not teaching Patricia is learning something new. Her latest ventures are agility training her Australian Cattle Dog, and herding lessons with her Border Collie. She is the wife of a retired Air Force officer and mother to three grown sons. At home you'll find her gardening, hiking, and enjoying the great outdoors in the company of a mixed pack.

Resources

Be a predator for resources.

- Keep your eyes and ears open to activities other faculty use that excite students and help them learn.
- Keep files of ideas.
- Go to conferences on teaching. Grab everything.
- Use ALL the resources at your own college. Most have a dedicated Center for Teaching and Learning filled with ideas from books, podcasts, videos, etc., and a faculty director to help you. Nearby colleges have guest speakers. Use it all.
- Check out YouTube, TED Talks, and other such sources. There are experts out there, talking!
- All the Big Ten have excellent on-line resources on college teaching. A few keystrokes and you are at a teaching/assessing buffet.

So get clever – hunt for tantalizing tips. If you have this frame of mind you will never go stale as a teacher.

BUT….

Don't go crazy. There is SO MUCH information, SO MANY great ideas, that you may feel the need to change many things every semester. This is the road to wearing baggy white clothes with arms that tie in the back. This book alone has a lot of sound ideas, but you can't reasonably adopt them all at once.

What is reasonable? Find some things that work for you and your students and repeat them. Then come up with two new formative assessments per semester and two new learning activities. Is it reasonable to also revise a handful of test items into a new format? Design one new rubric? That all sounds pretty manageable during a school year. If you keep this pace up, you will own quite a satisfying repertoire of teaching and assessing skills in just three or four semesters. Try to do too much all at once and teaching becomes a labor intensive, desperate kind of job. You want it to do more than pay your bills; teaching needs to feed your sense of meaning and purpose.

Be sure to recognize reality. You may not always be an "A" teacher. You may not have the time or skills yet to hit "A" marks on a daily basis. That's the way it is. Accept it. Keep trying. Keep improving. This really is a journey, and since a new class starts each semester, the journey keeps evolving.

Here are some topics and resources you may want to explore. I apologize in advance for any websites that go down before you find them. (Ah, the challenge of committing to print in a digital world.) Just google the essence of the topic and you'll find something similar.

Topics to Explore

Deep and Surface Learning
http://exchange.ac.uk/learning-and-teaching-theory-guide/deep-and-surface-approaches-learning.html

Reflective Judgment
http://www.umich.edu/~refjudg/reflectivejudgmentmodel.html
https://www.radford.edu/content/dam/departments/administrative/QEP/LessonIdeas/Reflective-judgment-model.pdf

Task Analysis
For a brief overview: http://www.usabilitynet.org/tools/taskanalysis.htm

Learning How to Learn
http://www.ibiblio.org/kuphaldt/socratic/doc/lett0045.pdf Fantastic article: If I'd Wanted to Study I Would Have Gone to a Real College

Bloom's Taxonomy
http://eduscapes.com/tap/topic69.htm – links to numerous Bloom sites and onward to critical and creative thinking
Significant Learning – L. Dee Fink is another curriculum/taxonomy guru well worth checking out. His site includes a free guide to course design.
http://www.deefinkandassociates.com/GuidetoCourseDesignAug05.pdf

Critical Thinking
http://www.criticalthinking.org/ This is a must-visit site, home to the critical thinking community and all those fantastic little books on CT.

Test Development

How to Write Better Tests – excellent article by the same name, practical and to the point

http://www.indiana.edu/~best/pdf_docs/better_tests.pdf

Best Practices in On-Line Teaching

http://www.uwec.edu/AcadAff/resources/edtech/upload/Best-Practices-in-On-line-Teaching-Strategies-Membership.pdf Hanover Research Report.
http://www.brown.edu/academics/professional/faculty/online/best-practices.php All large colleges seem to have recommendations for best practices.
This one from Brown University will start you out. There are many, many others.
Check out Purdue, University of Minnesota, and Indiana University.

Further Reading

Anderson, Lorin, and David R. Krathwohl (eds.). 2001. *A taxonomy for learning, teaching, and assessing: A revision of Bloom's Taxonomy of educational objectives.* Boston: Allyn & Bacon.

Angelo, Thomas A., and K. Patricia Cross. 2005. *Classroom assessment techniques: A handbook for college teachers*, rev. ed. Hoboken, NJ: John Wiley & Sons.

Bloom, Benjamin S. (ed.) 1956. *Taxonomy of educational objectives: The classification of educational goals.* New York: David McKay.

Brinkley, Alan, Esam El-Fakahany, Betty Dessants, Michael Flamm, Charles B. Forcey, Jr., Mathew L. Ouellett, Anderic Rothschild. 2011. *The Chicago handbook for teachers, second edition: A practical guide to the college classroom.* Chicago; University of Chicago Press.

Cohen, Dov, and Emily Kim, Jacinth Tan, Mary-Ann Winkelmes. 2013. A note-restructuring intervention increases students' exam scores. *College Teaching,* 61 (Summer), 95-99.

Jensen, Eric P. 2000. *Brain-based learning: the new science of teaching and training,* rev. ed. San Diego CA: The Brain Store.

McKeachie, Wilbert J., and Marilla Svinicki (eds.). 2013. *McKeachie's teaching tips: Strategies, research, and theory for college and university teachers, 14th ed.* Belmont, CA: Wadsworth Cengage Learning.

Meier, David. 2000. *The accelerated learning handbook: A creative guide to designing and delivering faster, more effective training programs.* New York: McGraw-Hill.

Paul, Richard, and Linda Elder. 2001. *The miniature guide to critical thinking: Concepts and tools.* Dillon Beach, CA: Foundation for Critical Thinking.

Pintrich, Paul R., and Dale H. Schunk. 2002. *Motivation in education: Theory, research, and applications.* Englewood Cliffs, NJ: Merrill.

Wigfield, Allan, and Jacqueline S. Eccles (eds.). 2001. *Development of achievement motivation.* Orlando, FL: Academic Press.

Wood, Robert, and Albert Bandura. 1989. Social cognitive theory of organizational management. *Academy of Management Review,* 14:361-384.

Woolfolk, Anita. 2013. *Educational psychology: Active learning edition. 12th ed.* New York: Pearson.

NOTES

Our two specialties

Practical books on Education	Focused on great ideas college teachers can implement immediately
Challenging, exciting books for middle and YA children	Our children and grandchildren will be running the world soon. Help them develop the thinking skills to ask questions, expect complexity, and see way beyond the simplistic "good guys" vs. "evil guys" paradigm that sometimes dominates mainstream discussion, books, and video games. Do you pre-read books before giving them to your children? Do you feel YA includes way too much "adult" material? We offer books in the adventure, fantasy, and science fiction genres that you will not have to pre-read. Our books really are age appropriate. Embedded inside each book are questions that spur deeper thinking about the material, the characters, and the difficult choices they must make. These start great discussions.

For a mindful, kinder world view

www.mixedpackpress.com